MONEY TALKS

Candid Conversations about Wealth in America

ROBERT KOPPEL

Dearborn Financial Publishing, Inc.®

This publication is designed to provide accurate and authoritative information in regard to the subject matter covered. It is sold with the understanding that the publisher is not engaged in rendering legal, accounting, or other professional service. If legal advice or other expert assistance is required, the services of a competent professional person should be sought.

Editorial Director: Cynthia A. Zigmund
Managing Editor: Jack Kiburz
Interior Design: Lucy Jenkins
Cover Design: Scott Rattray, Rattray Design
Typesetting: Jameson Blanchard

© 1999 by Robert Koppel

Published by Dearborn Financial Publishing, Inc.®

All rights reserved. The text of this publication, or any part thereof, may not be reproduced in any manner whatsoever without written permission from the publisher.

Printed in the United States of America

99 00 01 10 9 8 7 6 5 4 3 2 1

Library of Congress Cataloging-in-Publication Data

Koppel, Robert.
    Money talks: candid conversations about wealth in America / by Robert Koppel.
       p. cm.
    Includes index.
    ISBN 0-7931-2791-2
    1. Money—United States—Psychological aspects. I. Title.
HG222.3.K67 1998
305.5′234′0973—dc21   98-29918
                                                                                        CIP

Dearborn books are available at special quantity discounts to use as premiums and sales promotions, or for use in corporate training programs. For more information, please call the Special Sales Manager at 800-621-9621, ext. 4384, or write to Dearborn Financial Publishing, Inc., 155 N. Wacker Drive, Chicago, IL 60606-1719.

Money is better than poverty, if only for financial reasons.
—*Woody Allen*

Never steal more than you actually need, for the possession of surplus money leads to extravagance, foppish attire, frivolous thought.
—*Dalton Trumbo*

Never ask of money spent
where the spender thinks it went.
Nobody ever was meant
to remember or invent
what he did with every cent.
—*Robert Frost*

The best way to keep money in perspective is to have some.
—*Louis Rukeyser*

Money won't buy happiness, but it will pay the salaries of a large research staff to study the problem.
—*Bill Vaughan*

... remember, a billion dollars isn't worth what it used to be.
—*J. Paul Getty*

The darkest hour of a man's life is when he sits down to plan how to get money without earning it.
—Horace Greeley

Money is the barometer of society's virtue.
—Ayn Rand

I've got all the money I'll ever need if I die by four o'clock.
—Henny Youngman

He was so broke he couldn't even pay attention.
—Anonymous

Money is one of those human creations that make concrete a sensation, in this case the sensation of wanting, as a clock does the sensation of passing time. It is that double aspect of money, airy and substantial, that has fascinated all civilizations.
—John Buchan

Money is power, freedom, a cushion, the root of all evil, the sum of blessings.
—Carl Sandburg

Contents

Foreword   vii
Preface   xi
Acknowledgments   xiii

1. IT'S ONLY MONEY — 1
2. KEEPING SCORE: A Personal Tale — 15
3. I DON'T WANT TO TALK ABOUT IT / Judith McCue — 25
4. CRIME DOESN'T PAY / Matt Mahoney — 31
5. ART ENRICHMENT / Dorian Sylvain — 42
6. KISS: Keep It Simple, Stupid / Larry Rosenberg — 53
7. ALL THE PRESIDENT'S MEN / Rich Buendorf — 60
8. JAZZ WARRIOR / Kahil El'Zabar — 70
9. UNTIL DEATH US DO Part / Grant Jones — 77
10. ROCK AND SALVATION / Donna Hughes — 85
11. MONEY LOSSES / Ira Sapir — 92
12. REFLECTIONS ON A POND / Bernadine Dohrn — 100
13. RISKY BUSINESS / John Monasta — 108
14. YOU BE THE JUDGE / Michele Lowrance — 117
15. THE ULTIMATE BUZZ / Jim Nicodem — 125

CONTENTS

16. AS SIMPLE AS ABC / Kenny Dichter — 131
17. SALE DAYS / Joyce Rubin — 137
18. DRILLING FOR DOLLARS / Earl Augspurger — 146
19. MUTUAL FUNDS / Carole Ober — 150
20. THE PURSUIT OF PURPOSE / Abraham Twerski — 159
21. STOCKS AND PONDS / David Held — 168
22. POCKET CHANGE / Tom Cummins — 173
23. PERSONAL FINANCE / Howard Abell — 180
24. MAKING TOO MUCH MONEY / Steve Franklin — 187
25. COUNT ME IN / Michele Carbone — 194
26. NO SHORTCUTS / Paul Ciolino — 199
27. MAKING LOCOMOTIVES AND MONEY / Edward Kibblewhite — 206
28. AESTHETIC VALUES / Alan Koppel — 212
29. WORSHIPING THE ALMIGHTY DOLLAR / Joseph Morgan — 218
30. BELIEVING IS SEEING / Barbara Holt — 225
31. MONEY MATTERS: I Did It for the Money — 233

Index   247

Foreword

Economists have long sought to track the precise movement of capital. Among the legions of statistics of study is the *money supply,* or the amount of money circulating within various accounts across the nation. Abbreviated simply as "M," the figures are an astronomical indicator of our nation's favorite obsession. What follows in *Money Talks: Candid Conversations about Wealth in America* are the stories behind the statistics. This is the real story of M and its effect on the lives and personalities of 28 Americans.

Money usually is the focus of obsession but not so much honest, personal discussion. Like animals stockpiling food for the winter, our rhetorical exploration of money is persistently quantitative. Bookstores are brimming with innumerable ways to increase your net worth—stock market strategies, tightwad tips . . . it's all there. We've got money on our minds in our relentless dash for more cash.

Where does it go? Lavish luxuries? Much-needed medication? Egalitarian and indifferent, money is oblivious to the manner in which it is spent. During these golden years of the capitalist experiment, the choices we make surrounding money are indeed the manifestation of self-conception. More than any other resource, the allocation of our money clarifies our past and defines our future.

A worthy point: Money is inherently neither "good" nor "evil," rather simply a means toward an end. Affluence affords the material trappings of the day, and even Siddhartha would admit the road toward spiritual nirvana is greased with greenbacks.

In devising his groundbreaking "hierarchy of needs," A. H. Maslow tried to determine how humans seek happiness or fulfillment. The foundation is built firstly on the biogenetic demands of the human form: namely, hunger, shelter, thirst, and sex. Housing and nourishment make up a large percentage of most people's income, while sex has proved to be the "killer application" for the technological revolution that powers our economy to this day. One's ability to achieve the apex of Maslow's theory, *self-actualization,* is arguably correlated with cash. Money provides or denies us access to explore every nuance of a fulfilled life.

Rational humans have goals. We have wants. Our monetary resources give us permission to achieve those goals, to get what we want. Those who aspire to the material world should take great comfort in knowing that in contemporary capitalism there's not much that money can't buy. As you'll begin to understand from reading the stories within, those aren't necessarily the goals in which we are most interested.

Money has long moved beyond keeping up with the Joneses. When trillions of dollars traverse the globe with a keystroke, and water-cooler conversation is more focused on stocks than *Seinfeld,* how can we define our philosophical relationship with the almighty dollar? In an era of tremendous economic polarization, how can even the remotely affluent contextualize money within their ordinary lives?

So read on! Get to know the fascinating people Bob Koppel has unearthed. Individually, you'll begin to understand the lives, thoughts, and fortunes of a diverse group of representative individuals. Collectively, their experiences evidence the most subtle

FOREWORD

nuance of contemporary capitalism: the psychological relevance of money within our lives.

Man's needs are relatively slim. Shelter, food, and rest are essentially all we truly need to live. *Money Talks* is the story of everything else.

> —Jonathan Hoenig, host of Capitalist Pig Radio and a regular commentator on Public Radio International's *Marketplace*

Preface

We make money the old-fashioned way—we earn it.
—*Smith Barney advertising slogan*

Money. From its very origins to the present time, few objects have been so feverishly sought after, and there is virtually nothing human beings have not done in its name. People have lied, killed, cheated, speculated, loved, and died to obtain it. It has occasioned moral and religious strictures, been the source of violent national strife, and occupied an ongoing central focus in the daily lives of most people. Songs and plays have been written about money. Shakespearean sonnets and Stephen King novels have explored man's greed for it. Voltaire declared, "It is easier to write about money than to acquire it, and those who gain it make great sport of those who only know how to write about it."

Money Talks: Candid Conversations about Wealth in America explores this fascinating subject, concentrating on the psychological value and importance of money in our everyday lives. Interviews have been conducted with a wide variety of individuals of diverse social and educational backgrounds, cultures, ethnicities, religions, professions, and interests.

The interviews are set against a backdrop of broader economic, moral, and social attitudes to help probe how and why money makes the world go round; and, I hope, each offers a fine lens into our basic nature.

PREFACE

It is my goal in *Money Talks* to present a Studs Terkel–like investigation of people's attitudes and actions, as reported in their own words, adopted to secure money, and in so doing discover what they learned about it and themselves. The focus of this book is to reveal the economic and psychological value of money to the individual, rather than to describe the function and value of money in an anthropological or historical sense or its role in different cultures or societies. I believe most people will find the ideas and information presented here as thoughtful and reflective as the individuals who appear in these pages. I believe *Money Talks* also will serve as a valuable resource to assist people in their money-related decisions. As the old New England proverb says, "Dollars do better when they are accompanied by sense."

Acknowledgments

I wish to thank all the individuals who graciously agreed to be interviewed for *Money Talks*. Despite demanding schedules, each was generously forthcoming. I deeply appreciate their candor and insight into the role and meaning of money in their lives. Their perceptions serve as a reflecting pool for how we create value, enriching ourselves and society.

I would like to thank Mara Koppel for reading the original manuscript and for providing fine editing suggestions. Howard Abell's contribution also has proved invaluable. His comments and suggestions were most helpful. Thanks also go to my children, Lily and Niko, who have unwittingly given me a constant and consistent appreciation for the importance of money. Each day they remind me exactly what money can and cannot buy!

Finally, I would like to acknowledge the uncompromising support and wealth of ideas from my editor, Cindy Zigmund, and the entire staff of Dearborn Financial Publishing. Their encouragement throughout this project is warmly noted.

> **In these pursy times Virtue itself of vice must pardon beg.**
> —*Hamlet*

CHAPTER 1

It's Only Money

*I'm living so far beyond my income that we may almost
be said to be living apart.*

—e. e. cummings

Is there a more familiar question heard throughout the world than *How much does it cost?* In France they ask, *Combien est-ce?* In Germany, *Wievel kostet es?* In Italy, *Quanto costa? ¿Cuonto vale?* in Spain and Latin America. And in Russia, *Skok'ko eto stoit?*

Mark Twain observed, "Money is something you've got to make just in case you don't die." Adlai Stevenson revealed his feelings about money when he quipped, "There was a time when a fool and his money were soon parted, but now it happens to everybody!" Pablo Picasso expressed his conflicted attitude about wealth when he exclaimed, "I'd like to live like a poor man with lots of money."

The subject of money, like religion and sex, has occupied the intellectual curiosity of wise men since the dawn of time. The first traces of the development of money in the West begin with the ancient civilizations of Egypt and Mesopotamia, where there is ample historical evidence of strong monetary and commercial activity. In Genesis 37:28 we are presented with another reminder of a thriving trade that existed between buyers and sellers: "Then there passed by Midianites, merchant men, and they drew and lifted up Joseph out of the pit, and sold Joseph to the Ishmaelites for twenty pieces of silver, and they brought Joseph into Egypt."

Current scholarship suggests that money was not invented in a particular place at a particular time, but rather evolved in a multiplicity of forms for many purposes. As a medium of exchange, money has assumed a variety of forms dictated by cultural habits, social connections, successful experiences, and local acceptability. Money has been expressed as gold coins and bank notes, but also in more exotic forms: wampum, cowrie shells, whale's teeth, toucan feathers, salt, axes, knives, hides, iron, tobacco, cigarettes, liquor, cattle, rice, mahogany, and slaves. The money of the present and future is plastic and electrical impulses. The wide use of cattle as money in primitive times survives in the word *pecuniary*, which derives from the Latin *pecus*, meaning cattle.

In *Remembrances of Things Past*, Marcel Proust writes, "Material objects have in themselves no power, but since it is our practice to bestow power upon them . . ." This observation applies equally well to our discussion of money and how we value it. Consider the lottery ticket: one moment it is virtually worthless; the next it is drawn and declared the winner and is immediately deemed valuable. We have given money the power to transform someone's life forever! It seems to me quite clear that the essence of money does not lie in its statistics or numismatics, but rather in human attitudes and behavior: what we feel and think about it, what we are willing to trade for it, and what effect it has on our lives.

In *Frozen Desire*, James Buchan writes, "As a means, I saw that money was all but absolute: it could now realize every fantasy of creation or murder. And at that moment of extreme instrumentality, it was transforming once again: into an absolute end. Money was valued not for its power to convey wishes: rather it was the goal of all wishes. Money was enthroned as the God of our times."

As we approach the dawn of a new century there is still something of a feeling of psychological unease that is lingering in the last days of the 20th century. We are once again—for it is not entirely new—experiencing uncertainty about politics, the environment, and our economy. There is also a sense of loss of control with the constant attacks on familiar institutions: the family, religion, schools, tradition. We feel collectively as a society at the threshold of a new age of insecurity with the critical challenges posed by technological advance, globalization of markets, information overload, and the concentration and consolidation of wealth in the hands of a few multinational corporations and powerful private individuals. Money, of course, emerges as a likely culprit and perhaps ultimate cause for all our worries: the plausible villain and the single most influential agent negatively shaping our collective consciousness.

What we have here is not the straightforward moralizing attacks of the medieval church identifying money as the root of all evil, a fearsome sermon about its destructive influence on ecclesiastical and family values. For most of us, our concerns about money are far more complex and subtle in its implications. Intuitively we sense money is like plutonium: it provides a nuclear charge to our existence with the ever-present danger of reaching critical mass. But the dangers and exhilarations insinuate themselves with an almost benign neutrality. What I wish to convey here is that I believe for most of us, although we feel that money decidedly involves an ethical dimension, we think that on the whole it is probably good; that money is not diseased in the way it was thought to be by medieval clerics. It does not seriously affect our religious health! At the same time it is noteworthy that for most of us issues of salvation do not preoccupy our daily existence. We inhabit a far more complex universe; light years beyond the simplistic teaching that money, family, and religion cannot coexist in the real world as well as beyond any romantic notion that money is evil in an aesthetic sense; that any enterprise undertaken for monetary gain is tarnished in its purity. Money is no longer viewed as a serious enemy of thoughtful reflection, creative enterprise, or artistic expression. After all, this is the age of Bill Gates, Steven Spielberg, George Lucas, Michael Eisner, and Madonna. We live in a world of risk arbitrage and futures trading. Great basketball leaping ability can net athletes more money in a single year than robber barons accumulated in a lifetime. Moral choice and aesthetic integrity are just not worth what they used to be!

In many respects our culture has grown out of an age that lost faith in the "age of faith," reinventing itself into an age of money. But the money of our age is a very different kind of money. It is both powerful and intangible, which assigns to it qualities of mystery and paradox. Fortunes are made and lost overnight electron-like on stock markets and in foreign exchange trading around the world. Money has transformed itself from the solidity and weight of precious metal coins to the electronic impulses of financial lasers scurrying like cyberspace sperm cells in search of an egg.

Despite these significant changes in the physical properties of money from shell to coin to bank note to plastic to electronics, the fundamental functions of money have remained constant. Simply put, they are the following:

- To serve as a medium of exchange
- To act as a measure of value
- To serve as a standard of deferred payments (for loans or future transactions)
- To provide a convenient store of wealth

In other words, to have an asset function that provides liquidity.

An essential change in the concept of money that warrants our considered attention is the intangibility of something that exerts such a powerful effect on our lives. This is the first time in human history that the intangible has become a medium of exchange and a measure of value of the unimaginable. If you can afford it, it even has a price tag! Of course, purchasing the intangible in the past was the rarefied province of sovereigns and aristocrats. Prince Esterhazy could sponsor a Beethoven Mass or Shah Jahan build the Taj Mahal in memory of his beloved. And if a monarch possessed the "desire," his money could buy almost anything: even earth, air, fire, and water!

What I think is happening today that is markedly different is that money is becoming more human-like, assuming characteristics that in some sense are practically psychological. This is to say we find characteristics in money that we know to be true in ourselves: fluid, temporary, indifferent, emotional, generous, and unstable. As society inevitably develops greater consciousness of all things, so does it affect our concept of money, with one important twist. Today money has the same look and feel as our imagination itself: we possess our money quite literally not in our pockets but in our minds!

As a society, our concept of money is as often unclear as the many positive, negative, conflicting, contradictory, strange, funny, acerbic things that have been said to describe it. For example:

> Money, it turned out, was exactly like sex. You thought of nothing else if you didn't have it, and thought of other things if you did.
>
> —*James Baldwin*

> The chief value of money lies in the fact that one lives in a world in which it is overestimated.
>
> —*H. L. Mencken*

> A fool and his money are soon parted. What I want to know is how they got together in the first place.
>
> —*Cybil Fletcher*

> Always live within your income, even if you have to borrow money to do so.
>
> —*Josh Billings*

Get money first; virtue comes afterward.
—*Horace*

Seek wealth, it's good.
—*Ivan Boesky*

Today our attempts to understand money are much like an earlier generation's efforts to comprehend the paintings of Picasso and Braque: we try to view money from all possible perspectives all at once. However there is a critical difference: money is indifferent to its physical form and allows people not only to expand their physical possessions but the potential psychological freedom that that allows. Money has evolved to the level of pure sensation—sensation not only as a means, but as an end in itself. Money has thus been reinvented from a medium of desire to the object of all desire.

Throughout human history money has always taken on a form and could be understood in terms of the current orderly conception of man's place in society. Consider the following:

There are three faithful friends: an old wife, an old dog, and ready money.
—*Benjamin Franklin*

Money, which represents the prose of life, and which is hardly spoken of in parlors without an apology, is, in its effects and laws, as beautiful as roses.
—*Ralph Waldo Emerson*

Money is like manure. If you spread it around, it does a lot of good, but if you pile it up in one place, it stinks like hell.
—*Clint W. Murchison*

> Money is always there, but the pockets change.
> —*Gertrude Stein*

> If you want to know what God thinks of money, look at the people he gives it to.
> —*Shalom Alachem*

> Money is a good servant, but a bad master.
> —*Henry George Bohn*

> Mothers always tell you that honesty is the best policy, and money isn't everything. They're wrong about other things too.
> —*Mark Twain*

The more we try to conceptualize money through the lens of the past, the more paradoxical has become our understanding of it. This is in spite of explanation and control promised but never realized by the rise of monetary and economic theory. To cite only one example, consider the panic in Asian markets in the fall of 1997 and the futile efforts to save their currencies by central banks and southeast Asian governments. At the end of the 20th century, despite technological and intellectual advances, money remains a mysterious concept. The essential paradox is that money is at one and the same time viewed as the motivating agent of Western culture—a "fetish" of personal and corporate desire, and "immaterial" in the form it assumes and in the means of its acquisition. And so we are left with a fundamental question: How can something so elusive be so powerful?

As individuals, most of us often don't realize—or choose not to admit to ourselves—the influence our perception of money exerts on the quality of our daily lives. Our personal perspective on money has wide-ranging implications for how we value ourselves, our families, the nation, and the environment. It seems to me that in many ways money itself is the last taboo. This is not to say, of course, that money is a subject that does not routinely come into public view. Just the opposite is true! We are bombarded with consumerism and materialism from the moment our alarm clock rings (it has the manufacturer's name on it), to the second we fall asleep. Even our sheets and pillowcases proclaim who they are! After all, we live in a world of communicating products. We share our environment with polo horses, golden fleeces, and Nike swooshes—that cry out like hungry babies for our constant and immediate attention.

"Net worth" becomes a function of a particular car, house, tie, shoe, or purse—you name it! Psychological comfort is as close by as the right label! You're feeling low, but need to feel sexy. Forget Dr. Laura; you can have Ralph, Calvin, Giorgio, and Donna. Even his death doesn't prevent you from owning Gianni! You can have the "real thing" from "people who care" and remember, always "have it your way."

A recent clothing advertisement in *The New Yorker* magazine even attributed human traits to its garment. The copy reads: "A suit with a look as confident as your own." A shirt ad by a carriage trade manufacturer advises: "Handmade English shirts for gentlemen and ladies—when the papers want to know whose shirt you wear." An ad for the Waldorf Astoria confides: "The social register. Our guest book. People are always getting the two confused."

In recent years book titles about money have been proliferating like rabbits undergoing fertility injections. Consider just a few:

Your Money or Your Life
Die Rich and Tax Free
Die Broke
The Complete Idiot's Guide to Managing Your Money
A Girl Needs Cash
Ten Steps to Financial Success

The Nine Steps to Financial Freedom
8 Ways to Avoid Probate
The Seven Secrets of Financial Success
The Millionaire Next Door

Our individual confusion about money, ironically, is only exacerbated in this age of information. The carrot of double- and triple-digit investment returns is dangled out before us in the guise of seminars, tapes, and infomercials by a comical—although profitable—legion of financial sideshow barkers and confidence men.

Classified advertising of investment opportunities from a well-respected investment periodical revealed the following come-ons:

- Unconditionally guaranteed
- Buy a trading system too good to *sell!*
- Unlimited income potential
- The world's last great opportunity to build a large personal fortune (selling magazine subscriptions)

My favorite, though, was this one that was advertising, guess what, a money book. The copy reads: "You are biologically and culturally wired [in quotes] to lose a great deal of money in your lifetime. Chances are you'll self-destruct within a year. You could lose everything because you've ignored this warning. Act Now."

The last ad I would like to mention appeared in the September 1996 issue of *Technical Analysis of Stocks and Commodities*, a periodical favored by professional stock, foreign exchange, and futures traders. When I first saw this advertisement I had to reread it several times to convince myself that I hadn't picked up a sci-fi entomology digest! There is a picture of a New York water bug—the kind of insect that prevents hard-boiled New York apartment dwellers from ever going into a basement laundry. The copy above the picture leads with "Go ahead and just smash it." Then it poses this thoughtful question: "Ever try to kill cockroaches with household insecticide? They always come back, don't they? Ever try to make money in the markets using conventional trading systems and charting programs? Good luck . . ." The ad then goes on to explain why "Nature's Pulse [I'm not kidding] Software is different and warrants you shelling out big bucks!" The ad concludes with these confident words: "So the next time you hear about some dynamic new trading software or methodology, remind yourself that in order to kill a cockroach, you have to think like one. Not a pretty thought. But who cares—as long as you make money."

I'm reminded of three old Wall Street adages:

1. Choose your investments the way porcupines make love—very carefully!
2. It is not the return *on* my investment that I'm worried about, it is the return *of* my investment.
3. If stock market experts were so expert, they would be buying stocks, not selling advice.

The essential question still remains in the face of this omnipresent, and often crude, materialism that constantly points out individual insufficiency in areas as wide ranging as appearance and outlook to family health care and portfolio enhancement. How are we to clarify our understanding of the meaning of money? How can we assign certainty to the value of what we think and feel about money and what effect it has on our lives?

I believe that it is this taboo of speaking about money in just these terms that prevents the clarification of its meaning in our lives. Again, everyone speaks about money, but mostly in impersonal or theoretical terms. I have a friend who is a psychoanalyst who confided in me that he has clients who will speak in detail to him about the most traumatic moments of their lives, their sexual fantasies and predilections—down to the number and quality of their orgasms. But ask them to talk about their money and they shut down like clams!

Money presents itself as the ultimate Rorschach test of individual desire. Money can be seen and used as a generous instrument of creativity and vision, or as a consuming agent of ruinous greed and self-absorption. It is just this psychological aspect of money that compelled me to learn more.

I began to seriously consider the following:

- Where does money get its value?
- How can an inanimate object so indifferent to our wants and desires have so much power over us?
- Why do we allow ourselves to both define and be defined by it?
- How does our attitude about money affect the clothes we buy, the homes we live in, and the cars we drive?
- What can we do as individuals to gain a better understanding of money so that we can bring added "value" to our lives.

I approached my editor, Cindy Zigmund of Dearborn Financial Publishing, with the idea for *Money Talks*. The great baseball Hall of Famer Honus Wagner once said, "There's not too much to playing baseball, if you can play baseball." That pretty much sums up my feelings about Cindy's editing. I have had other editors; I can tell in a Chicago instant the difference between those who can and can't play ball! Cindy is the kind of editor who, once she hears your idea and likes it, and is convinced your proposal has more merit than your need for an advance, just "jumps on it."

We both felt that although there were scores of books written about money (several of which Cindy had edited), that there was little if anything published on the psychology of money, focusing on interviews with a wide variety of people. My idea then was to contact a broad cross section of individuals of diverse backgrounds, professions, and interests, and ask them some very specific questions that would shed light on this subject. I wanted to know the following:

- What is your earliest memory of money?
- What was your family's attitude toward money?
- As you were growing up, what were your thoughts about money?
- As a youngster, did you feel it was important for you to have a lot of money?
- As you were growing up, what fantasies did you have about money?
- Do you believe money is the root of all evil or the sum of all blessings?
- How would you characterize your current experience/relationship with money?
- To what extent do you feel others define you in terms of how much money you have?
- To what extent do you believe you define yourself in terms of your net worth? And why?
- How much money do you think is enough?
- What is most valuable to you? Why?
- In your personal system of values, what do you think is the ultimate purpose of money?
- What is it about money do you think that gets us so "hung up"?
- To what extent do you think money has significantly affected your quality of life?
- Can you think of an important (or defining) experience in your life where you felt you reached a better understanding of the "true value" of money?
- What do you think is the most important thing that you learned about yourself relative to your understanding of money?

As I began telling friends about my project, I was amazed at the strength of the general interest in this subject. I have published five books previously and never before experienced such enthusiasm or the desire to be interviewed. I even received a call from an estranged relative who thought this book "fit him to a tee" and was "just up his alley."

I realized at that point I would have to closely screen the interviews and get as broad a range of subjects as possible. They are not necessarily representative of the general population, nor in truth was this my intention. What I had hoped to achieve, and think I have, is to present a diverse group of accomplished people from all social, religious, and ethnic backgrounds who have thought-provoking things to say about the meaning of money.

Among the many people I interviewed are an elected family court judge, astronomer, artist, musician, psychiatrist, international journalist, president of a financial services company, professional portfolio manager, trader, art historian, Secret Service agent assigned to President Clinton, race horse owner, housewife, dentist, professional gambler, secretary, investment book author, record producer, politician, Italian count, minister, rabbi, geneticist, and gallery owner. I am convinced that their observations about the role of money in their lives strengthens our understanding of how we assign value in ours as well as offering a fine lens into our human nature.

> The nicest thing about money is that it never clashes with anything I wear.
>
> —*Myron Cohen*

> When it is a question of money everybody is of the same religion.
>
> —*Voltaire*

Money is a very excellent servant but a terrible master.

—P. T. Barnum

Early to bed and early to rise, 'til you make enough money to do otherwise.

—*Automobile bumper sticker*

If anything seems to be a constant in the history of money, it is surely the complaints of the moralists against the apparently ruinous effects of money on human culture and society.

—*Jonathan Williams*

CHAPTER 2

Keeping Score
A Personal Tale

> Money isn't important, it's just keeping score.
> —*Wall Street adage*

Heavyweight boxing champion Joe Louis once said, "I don't like money actually, but it quiets my nerves." This Yogi Berra–like assessment could well characterize my ambivalence toward money: an on-again, off-again love affair that nearly ruined my life on more than one occasion!

I grew up in New York City in a solid middle-class family that still possessed strong memories of the hardships imposed by the Great Depression. Among my uncles and aunts were doctors, lawyers, businesspeople, teachers, artists, and even a state supreme court justice. Money was a subject that was rarely spoken about but, like a feeling of plenty after a holiday dinner, was always at the forefront of my consciousness.

My grandfather, a descendant of Talmudic scholars, was a penniless immigrant at the turn of the century who at 50 was able to retire because of wise investments. He lived to be 99 years old, never having to work another day in his life. He exercised the strongest influence on my youth, and what I learned from him was quite clear: The ultimate purpose of money is to help those less fortunate. My grandfather's life revolved around the synagogue and performing "good works." Not once do I recall him speaking of money except as it related to charitable acts. I do, however, remember his constant reminders to all his grandchildren of the four key passages of the "Ethics of our Fathers" from the Talmud, on whose principles a person could build a meaningful life:

1. Who is wise? The one who learns from everyone.
2. Who is strong? The one who conquers his/her own inclinations.
3. Who is respected? The one who respects all of God's creations.
4. Who is rich? The one who is content with his/her lot.

My parents' attitude toward money was more ambivalent. They shared my grandfather's philanthropic beliefs, but declined to live the kind of life he had chosen for himself: a simple, no-frills search for daily meaning at the expense of daily bread! At the age of 12 I can remember my mother presiding over a mysteriously celebratory family dinner in which she announced our mortgage had been paid off. I didn't quite get what the fuss was all about at the time, but what came through was unmistakable: having money was a good thing.

My own confused attitude toward money is partially reflected in the different careers of my parents. My father was a successful businessman who was always looking for ways to expand the family business he had started from scratch with his brother and sisters and my mother, who divided her time between teaching French literature and working for every charity and liberal cause known to man (and woman).

We lived in large houses—one for the winter and one at the shore for the summer, drove in luxury automobiles, and my brother and I attended private schools. It was in many ways a privileged life, but it also was one that was founded on a love/hate relationship with money. Money bought Cadillacs and Lincolns, but it also brought about the deterioration of one's values. It was the moral equivalent of a highly caloric, richly saturated fat-laden diet

KEEPING SCORE: A PERSONAL TALE

for monetary weight watchers; a serious threat to one's moral health!

At the age of 20 money fascinated me, but I was still confused. I had worked summers and after school to earn enough money to afford a brand new Austin Healy 3000 roadster. Guilty about my material possessions, I declared to myself, for once and for all, that I would reject the importance of money and lead a "different kind of life." (I say this now with embarrassment. Such a decision ignores Marcel Proust's famous words, "All permanent decisions are made in a state of mind that is destined to change.") I announced to my father that I would have no part in his textile business and shocked him still further when I told him I had changed my college major from political science to existential philosophy. Of course this was the '60s, man, and all you needed was enough "bread" to buy your favorite books (Sartre, Kierkegaard, and Marcuse) and get the Beatles' and Stones' latest releases.

After college I became a VISTA volunteer and worked in the inner cities of Cleveland, Ohio, and Buffalo, New York. I was mesmerized and appalled by the conditions in which I saw people living. These were good, hardworking, decent people who, through no fault of their own, but because of years of racism and neglect, found themselves inhabiting a hostile world of monetary deprivation. It was a world where money made a difference and if you didn't have it, your children went without and nobody cared! This must sound somewhat disingenuous in our postcynical, Clinton-Jones-Lewinsky, 1990s political landscape of "been there, done that." What I'm trying to express is my then-continuing personal struggle to understand the role of money in my life and in the lives of others. What I observed and felt viscerally was this: If you had money you possessed choices; if you didn't, not only would you be assigned to a perilous existence, but you would be defined as "subhuman." Money was much more than just keeping score!

All told I worked for about seven years in the inner city, in some of the toughest schools in southeast Bronx and Harlem. I had the opportunity to interact with children and parents, community leaders, politicians, businesspeople, and school administrators. I got to see firsthand how some of the "meek" of this earth are constantly caught, like a junked car, in a metal compactor between a thick impassive wall of moneyed interests, self-important "leaders," emotionally charged rhetoric, and malignant neglect.

All of this, however, could not shake my youthful idealism. I took a position as a midlevel researcher for a prestigious New York firm that concentrated on conducting government- and foundation-supported research in the areas of education, child abuse, and age discrimination. I published our findings and presented papers to professional organizations and federal agencies in Washington. Once again I was stunned at not only the waste of money by researchers and government officials, but the extreme need for money for credible programs. All of this took place against the backdrop of an industry standard of dragging its feet when it came to delivering meaningful studies. I was once severely chided by my boss, an industrial psychologist who was the product of a military academy, for arriving at a conclusion. I was told: "Don't you realize we are not in the business of making recommendations; our business is to generate new hypotheses for future funding." I had had enough of the ethical not-for-profit sector.

At this point my personal understanding about money was at a new low. However, my intellectual fascination with it was at an all-time high. In 1976 my artist wife and I moved to Chicago with a "greed is good" attitude and an amorphous ambition "to make it big." We had seen enough of the do-gooders and were ready to join the first ranks of the legion of free enterprise! Two years earlier my younger brother had moved to Chicago where he was working in the financial district as a commodities broker. A meteoric rise in the livestock market transformed Alan overnight into a millionaire. He traded in his one-bedroom West Side apartment next to the "L" tracks and ensconced himself in Highland Park, one of Chicago's ritzier suburbs. In the de rigueur North Shore manner, the house featured a swimming pool, tennis court, and a garage stocked with luxury automobiles. On a lark, at my brother's request, I spent a day with him at work, observing his operations on the trading floor.

My first impression was that the floor resembled the Great Barrier Reef, a virtual kaleidoscopic swell of activity with traders, exchange employees, and runners color-coded in aggressive neon shades, moving about with all the single-mindedness of the *Starship Enterprise;* a teeming, self-contained financial environment where only the most well-adapted life forms survive. It was a world of men and women who were committed with unwavering devotion to their ultimate quest: the ongoing crusade to make lots of money and spend it on every kind of imaginable extravagance. It was at one and the same time a vulgar capitalistic vision of wasted resources and ambition, and the ideal and epitome of what everybody wants. It was an electrified world of unlimited possibility and gold fever, a dream factory where a single well-calculated decision could change one's life forever.

From the first instant that I observed this complex theater of money with its elaborate stage sets and performers, I wanted to become a member of this powerful financial pageant. What appealed to me so viscerally was neither the blue-collar atmosphere nor the custom white-collar rewards. The appeal was having the opportunity to play high-stakes chess with immensely talented individuals whose litmus test for success was easily understood and respected: brains, guts, and timing. I found it exhilarating to spend each day in the company of men and women who combined physical athleticism and psychological discipline with intellectual agility and grace under fire. We shared a feverishly competitive, clearly focused, no-excuses environment.

Ironically, I discovered a greater sense of personal honor and integrity in this world than I had ever observed before among the not-for-profit crowd. In a given day financial products worth trillions of dollars change hands on the trading floor: everything from corn and cattle to U.S. Treasury bonds and foreign currencies. Trades are concluded with a facial gesture, a hand signal, or a nod. A person's word is his or her bond. This is not to say, of course, that the trading world doesn't have its share of bad apples; it certainly does. But in general the trading floor's engine is trust. Thousands of traders around the globe trust each other to honor moneyed promises for tangible commodities, precious metals, interest rates, and currencies, based on two monosyllabic words: *buy* or *sell.*

At 40 I had made millions in the market. My days consisted of buying and selling everything from British pounds sterling to pork bellies. (I mention these two because on the trading floor it is not uncommon for orders of the one to be confused with orders of the other. The symbol for "British"—as it's known—is BP, whereas the symbol for "bellies" is PB.)

I was one of the largest market makers on the trading floor and often traded "limit position size"—the largest position size allowable by federal law for a commodity trader. I felt invulnerable, a not-uncommon—although lethal—feeling among traders. In my mind I was the prince of the city, the king of the mountain. I had the Midas touch: I knew it and so did everyone else.

My life consisted of embracing risk: making it my friend and getting paid handsomely for the effort. An old trading expression states "nobody is bigger than the market." Inherent in that phrase is the idea that nobody is smarter than the market. In short, sooner or later the law of averages will catch up with you! I developed my personal appreciation of this fact not from reading it in an investment book but rather as a result of nearly losing everything for which I had worked. Gone in what felt like a money avalanche were almost all the material trappings of a successful life: money, houses, cars—you name it! My grandfather was once again right: everything we truly learn or understand in life creates in us a deeper sense of our own humility. At 42, I was definitely humbled.

KEEPING SCORE: A PERSONAL TALE

The odd thing is, along with this radical change of monetary fortune, came a huge, unexpected, sigh of relief. It was a very difficult and psychologically confusing period in my life. My family was faced with financial pressures they had never known before: it seemed like overnight we went from Chateaubriand to chateau Spam. The congresspeople and senators who just months ago called my wife and me inviting us to dinner parties in their homes coincidentally seemed to lose our phone number just as our fortunes were going south. The legion of sycophants and hangers-on who routinely appeared at our door was replaced by an army of bill collectors. There also were no more invitations to fund-raisers, celebrity parties, gallery openings, and charity events. I was either asked to resign or my name was removed from charitable and civic boards on which I served. When word gets out you have "money-AIDS," nobody wants to catch it!

In the ensuing years I have had the opportunity to analyze my understanding of money in light of all the events and experiences I have mentioned. In addition, in the books that I previously published I was able to study the thoughts and behavior of successful individuals in the financial arena to learn how they internalize their experience. In so doing I wrote extensively about personal motivation, belief, focus, discipline, confidence, and optimism. Then, as now, I try to write about issues that provide me with a better understanding of myself. This attitude is not born of selfishness; I just believe that this way there is something in it for everyone!

I am convinced now that in my system of values the ultimate purpose of money is to enhance or benefit from the experience of others. For me it is both a responsibility and an obligation. I also am convinced that I needed to lose my money in order to find its proper role in my life. Money is not only a medium of monetary value, but an expression of personal values.

It is easy to get distracted in life—to veer off a clear path or lose your way entirely. And money is a very poor compass. Its gravitational pull can take you to far-off destinations from which there may never be a road back. Fortunately this was not the case for me. Money has unquestionably had a significant effect on the quality of my life, but not in the way you might think. I realize now that all the trappings of wealth—houses, cars, boats, couture—were other people's scorecard of my success.

More than 2,000 years ago Greek philosophers concluded that more than anything else, the actions of men and women are motivated by the desire to seek happiness. Everything that we do and strive for—beauty, power, money—is "valued" only because we are committed to an expectation that it will make us happy. Much has changed in the intervening two millennia. Our understanding of ourselves and the universe has expanded beyond belief. The ancient gods of Greece are mere cartoons compared to the powers humankind now possesses. And yet one could easily argue we have made little progress in better understanding how to attain happiness and profoundly enhancing the quality of our lives.

In *Flow: The Psychology of Optimal Experience,* Mihaly Csikszentmihalyi writes: "Despite the fact that we are now healthier and grow to be older, despite the fact that even the least affluent among us are surrounded by material luxuries undreamed of even a few decades ago (there were few bathrooms in the palace of the Sun King, chairs were rare even in the richest medieval houses, and no Roman emperor could turn on a TV set when he was bored), and regardless of all the stupendous scientific knowledge we can summon at will, people often end up feeling that their lives have been wasted, that instead of being filled with happiness their years were spent in anxiety and boredom."

My search for happiness was misdirected by the gravitational pull of money. Ironically, the more I had, the less I felt fulfilled. The more control that I believed would be forthcoming, the less I experienced. In short, I did not feel as though I was a participant in the real content of my own life. This is not to say one needs to experience a cataclysmic event in his/her life to arrive at this realization. But I do feel one needs to be true to an authentic vision of oneself

KEEPING SCORE: A PERSONAL TALE

in a way where one is not merely passive or receptive. That is why I believe the act of accumulation or acquisition, in and of itself, is in the end so empty. Personal fulfillment is not ultimately determined by external agencies—what we see, feel, or do is affected but not controlled by conditions outside of ourselves. In the last analysis, happiness is the result of our ability to cultivate and master our own inner experience.

In *Man's Search for Meaning,* Viktor Frankl, the Austrian psychologist who had survived a Nazi concentration camp, warns: "Don't aim at success—the more you aim at it and make it a target, the more you are going to miss it. For success, like happiness, cannot be pursued, it must ensue . . . as the unintended side effect of one's personal dedication to a course greater than oneself." What I discovered is what I had known all along but refused to acknowledge as my truth: a meaningful life is not the result of good fortune or random chance. It cannot be bought with money or ordained into existence through the accumulation of luxury assets or the power money commands. My discovery, in truth, was one that people have been aware of since the dawn of time; but we inhabit a world of too many distractions, too much information, and we place too little value on the subjective experience of the individual. Robert Pirsig observed in *Zen and the Art of Motorcycle Maintenance,* "The truth knocks on the door and you say, 'Go away I'm looking for the truth.' And so it goes away."

In the chapters that follow we will discover the role of money in the lives of each of the individuals whom I interviewed, how the quality of their lives was affected or shaped by the importance of money, and whether the possession or the lack of money inhibited or enhanced their personal and professional lives. Most importantly, we will explore what they learned about themselves in terms of bringing value into their individual experiences.

And the end of all our exploring will be to arrive where we started and know the place for the first time.

—*T. S. Eliot, "Little Gidding"*

CHAPTER 3

I Don't Want to Talk About It

Judith McCue

MS. JUDITH MCCUE teaches the Great Books program to teachers and believes that "nice people do not talk about money."

Q: Judith, what is your earliest memory of money?

JUDITH: Getting pocket money as a kid, the equivalent of a quarter, I suppose.

Q: What was your feeling about money. Did you think it had some special property or would you say your attitude was more one of indifference?

JUDITH: That's interesting because it was a combination of both. I really was brought up to believe that money is only good for what it can be used for. It has no intrinsic value. I was taught that money didn't matter, so I feel very much all the time in America like a babe in the woods. When it comes to money I'm just constantly impressed by how much Americans know about how this stuff works. . . . My father, who was in real estate, had the opportunity many times to become very wealthy. He used to say that the only thing that's more useless than your first million is your second million.

Q: Where did you grow up?

JUDITH: Australia. It was a particularly blessed time, because you actually didn't need to be wealthy to have an extremely good lifestyle. So it was easy to be blasé about money.

Q: How would you characterize your family's attitude toward money?

JUDITH: Contradictory, like a lot of people, I suppose. I mean, it was certainly important. But there were other things that were far more important. For instance, time was valued as much more significant than money. I think that still is very much an Australian value. Given the choice, Australians will not work if they can have leisure time.

Q: Judith, you've lived and worked in the states for 12 years. How do you relate to the value that Americans place on money?

JUDITH: I've tried to work that one out for myself. The only conclusion I can come to is that in America, you really only have two choices, two ways to go. You either get ahead or you go down. There's no middle ground here where you can tread water. In America that's looked down upon. You've got to get ahead! There is a stigma attached to you here that you don't find in Australia or Europe if you don't have money.

Q: Does that provide a conflict for you?

JUDITH: Sure there's a tension, but it's fascinating to me. I'm just constantly trying to understand it, a bit like you in a sense. This total obsession with money. The cash value of things is what seems to matter, not the intrinsic value. Yes, I'm very fascinated by that!

Q: Judith, do you think people define you by how much money you have?

JUDITH: I try not to think about it because I couldn't care less. It doesn't seem to be something worth thinking about.

Q: As you were growing up, did you have any particular thoughts or fantasies about money?

JUDITH: No, not about money itself. About wealth perhaps, in a philosophical or anthropological sense. But the thoughts weren't necessarily attached to money.

Q: You studied cultural anthropology and economics at Cambridge, is that right?

JUDITH: Yes.

Q: How does that relate to your personal interest in money?

JUDITH: Oh, perfectly. It's all theoretical. It's all philosophical. It has nothing to do with keeping a household budget. Bob, this is another interesting point. Economic theory is something entirely different in England from economics in the United States. There it's philosophy; here it's business studies. Even the way economic development is used. Here it is real estate and building houses. It's not used like that in Britain. So, this too was something else I had to find out.

Q: Judith, your personal interest in economics was more an interest of the mind, more philosophical. Is that what you're saying?

JUDITH: Yes. It's always philosophical rather than practical.

Q: It is interesting that you went into that area of study, considering you had very little practical interest in money.

JUDITH: Yeah, and I can't keep a balance sheet, nor do I want to anyway. At Cambridge, if you wanted data, you just hired somebody to do it for you. It's not a skill that's particularly desirable. Use a calculator, or a person who can count. The important thing is how you think about the problem!

Q: Judith, when you arrived in the United States, what was your reaction to the emphasis placed here on money?

JUDITH: Quite honestly, complete lack of comprehension. I found it to be totally perplexing. I found it very strange that people in this country, even ordinary everyday people, seem to have such a familiarity and conversance with money. And also that money is treasured as an entity in itself. That's what I don't understand—money as an end in itself. That's very odd!

Q: If you were to think about a particular metaphor for money, what do you think it would be?

JUDITH: Therapy. I think in American society, money is therapy. It's comforting. It's like mother's milk. You know, when I'm at my most stressed and I've got more bills to pay than I can deal with or think about, what else is there to do? I go shopping!

Q: So, do you feel you've been well socialized into the money values of our country?

JUDITH: Yes and no, because I still can't decide to do something just for the money. My life would be a lot simpler if I could.

Q: How has your current work shaped or affected your personal concept of money?

JUDITH: I think I probably do what I do because I'm very incompetent with money. I mean, I work with books. I train people how to think. I conduct training courses for teachers, demonstrating how to approach literature, how to teach the Great Books. It involves learning how to interpret, which comes down to how to ask questions. How do you ask questions that will make your students think? It's very hard.

Q: It sounds Socratic in its method.

JUDITH: It is based on the Socratic method. American teachers have a lot of trouble with it. There is one other thing about money that I think is very interesting in this country. I don't think, in general, that Americans enjoy the sheer physical sensation or pleasure of money. Because pleasure here is something that is taboo. You can't have too much pleasure in this culture. You know, I'm sure this has been said by a thousand people before, but America is very puritanical. The historical background shapes the current attitudes. I think that's very interesting. I mean, we routinely see people with tons of money, but they're always unhappy. It's almost as if these people have to be unhappy. They have to be alcoholics. Their marriages have to be on the rocks or their kids have to be drug addicts. It's not enough just to have the money and enjoy it. That's not allowed. You have to be suffering.

Q: How do you make sense of that?

JUDITH: It has a lot to do with the way Americans perceive pleasure. This is still a very straitlaced country. People feel guilty about having a lot of fun. Everyone goes to bed at 9 o'clock, and they're tired all the time!

Q: Perhaps that's why so much mistaken emphasis is placed on money, because ultimately there's just so much pleasure you can get from it! What do you really value?

JUDITH: What do I really value?

Q: That's a big question.

JUDITH: Yeah, it's like "What's the meaning of life?" Well, you've got a year or two! But in shorthand, really crisp shorthand, I would say this: I value ideas, I value goodness in other people and of course my family.

Q: How would you currently describe your relationship with money.

JUDITH: Nonexistent!

Q: It doesn't fit into the life of the mind?

JUDITH: Well, my relationship with money is disastrous in a word. No matter what I do, I can never do enough to make enough to not have to think about it. And that would be the ideal, but of course that's not possible. I hate it. I really do.

Q: Judith, as it relates to your understanding of money, what is the most important thing you learned about yourself?

JUDITH: I try not to think about it, because it's such dreadful stuff. It generates in me an enormous amount of stress. I just don't want to think about money. I'm very good at putting things aside in a little pile and then dealing with them later. And six months later, you go back, and if you're lucky, the pile will have evaporated. It has gone away. But to answer your question, Bob, I want someone else to deal with it. I want someone else to pay the bills. I want someone else to balance the checkbook. It's all dreadfully boring.

Q: So basically what you've learned is that it's boring and you don't want to deal with it?

JUDITH: I'll think about it in a philosophical, sociological, political, or economic sense. But I find the day-to-day stuff soul-destroying. So why do it? Life's too short.

Q: I'm sorry if I made you feel uncomfortable. I was watching your reaction to some of these questions and I have the feeling that talking about money is very anxiety provoking for you.

JUDITH: Yes, well you see, I didn't realize until you started asking these questions, how inefficient I am at really thinking about money, and it touches all kinds of chords.

Q: So, what's your reaction to that?

JUDITH: I don't want to talk about money!

CHAPTER 4

Crime Doesn't Pay

Matt Mahoney

MR. MATT MAHONEY, 39, is a criminal defense attorney in Chicago. Prior to that he was a prosecutor for the Cook County State Attorney's office.

▼

Q: Matt, what is your earliest memory of money?

MATT: I think the earliest memory of money goes back to when I was six or seven. I received a share of stock from my grandfather and I asked my parents what it meant. They told me that the stock represented money, but I still didn't understand why I couldn't spend it.

Q: So how did you deal with that?

MATT: Well, I wanted to spend it on candy, but my parents told me I couldn't. I thought, "Wow, this money really sucks!"

Q: You thought money was a pretty perplexing thing at that point, right?

MATT: Yes, I did. Perplexing and frustrating.

Q: What was your family's attitude toward money?

MATT: I don't know exactly how to describe it in a short way. We were not wealthy and we were not poor. My father worked for the Central Intelligence Agency and we lived in foreign countries. In many of the places that we lived in we had a house, servants, and cars supplied by the government. We did our shopping on military bases and that sort of thing. So I really never had a particular concept of being poor or wealthy. Although there were times in some countries where we would see the lives of the indigenous peoples and realize that in comparison to our way of life, theirs was quite different.

Q: Did you spend any part of your childhood in one country for an extended period of time?

MATT: I was born in Mexico and my family spent a number of years in South Africa.

Q: So most of your childhood was spent in South Africa?

MATT: Yes. And traveling to other countries. England, Spain, Mexico, and the Caribbean—places like that.

Q: As you were growing up, what were your thoughts about money?

MATT: I liked it and wanted more of it. It seemed to me to be a means to an end.

Q: Did you feel it was important to have a lot of money?
MATT: Yes.

Q: Why is that?
MATT: I wanted as much as you could get. The more money you had the more things you could get.

Q: You mentioned that when you were living in some of these foreign countries that you observed the way the indigenous peoples were living. Did these experiences instigate any feelings of social concern or in any way create in you an appreciation of the positive as well as the negative aspects of money?

MATT: I recall one incident in particular. We were on a ship and we had stopped at the island of Haiti. I imagine I was 11 or 12 years old at the time. There were natives selling carved wooden figures. My father had told me that if I saw something that I liked, I should bargain. He said, "You don't just pay the price asked." As we were leaving, something occurred that still stands out in my memory. I had been speaking to this one Haitian about two carved bookends. I had been negotiating with him. We hadn't come to an agreement. I was still new to negotiating.

Q: A skill you would need to have later on in your life.

MATT: Exactly. And I remember this was my first experience where I was negotiating money in exchange for an object. I believe I was offering 50 cents and the Haitian man was asking a dollar fifty. In the middle of our back-and-forth, my father said, "Come on, we've got to go." So I said to the man, "OK, thanks. I'll see you later." I remember him following along beside us as we walked down to the pier saying, "75 cents, okay 60 cents, okay 45 cents." I remember the look of desperation on his face and feeling that these were objects that I really didn't even want. I was just bargaining for the sake of bargaining. At first it had been fun, but I soon realized this was pretty serious stuff. It made me ask myself, "What is this person's life really like?"

Q: You became aware that money really did have a very serious dimension and that the lack of it could make a person feel desperate. Is that it?

MATT: Yes, because the Haitian definitely wanted that money and it represented something close to subsistence. He needed the money in a literal sense!

Q: Matt, I think the idea of desperation provides a perfect transition for you to talk about some of the cases that you have been involved in as a prosecutor and now as a defense attorney. Would you talk about your professional role and how it relates to your current understanding of money?

MATT: What I have observed, Bob, is not so much desperate people in the sense of Jean Valjean in *Les Miserables*. I have not seen people committing egregious crimes for a loaf of bread. It is more instances of pure greed; people stealing money not to feed their starving children and not to put a roof over their heads. But instead looking to have a luxury car or fancy clothes, that sort of thing. It is an ugly, egotistical—rather than desperate—kind of greed.

Q: Can you think of a particular case that you worked on that illustrates this?

MATT: Sure. I remember one woman in particular who stands out in my mind. She was an Arab woman who was married to a businessman. Her husband owned a candy factory on the South Side of Chicago and he was fairly well off. She was having an affair with a mob wannabe. Not a real mob guy! He was just sort of on the fringes. During the course of their affair, her boyfriend was busted for cocaine possession. He didn't want to go to jail and—I should add the obvious—he wasn't a particularly nice fellow to begin with! As soon as he was in police custody he started trying to wiggle his way out of going to jail. He told the police, "I know a woman who's trying to have her husband killed." Of course the cops' ears perked up and they listened to his story. According to the boyfriend, the wife couldn't divorce the husband for two reasons. First, the divorce was unacceptable in her culture: she had two or three children that she didn't want to lose. Second, and more importantly, she didn't want to lose the income from his candy factory. Because she believed the boyfriend to be a mob person, she asked him to find her a hit man to kill her husband.

So the boyfriend tells this to the police officers to get himself out of the cocaine beef and the police officers come to me for a wire tap warrant, which is judicial permission to tape-record. We made some predicate telephone calls and we got judicial permission. We wired up an undercover police officer who was posing as Tony the Hit Man and he was put in contact with the wife. They met in a parked car in a Chicago neighborhood during the middle of a snowstorm. She gave him $5,000 in cash and a detailed description of her husband. She also wrote down his daily activities, which she listed on a cocktail napkin.

One of the things that the officer said to the woman while he was posing as the hit man was, "Now are you sure you want me to kill him? I could just break his legs to teach him a lesson." From an evidentiary standpoint, we wanted to have her words on tape in no uncertain terms stating she wanted him killed. Her response was, "No, I want him dead. Dead, dead, dead, just dead!" At that point the officer asked, "Well, do you want me to say something to him before I kill him? Like 'This one is from your wife,' to which the wife responded, "Oh, no. God, no. I don't want him coming back and spooking me."

She was arrested at the scene because the crime of solicitation to commit murder for hire consists solely of asking someone to kill and paying him money; no injury to anyone needs to occur. She was taken to the Oak Lawn police station where I interviewed her. As I played the tape recording for her, I was explaining her legal rights and asking her version of what had happened. She looked at me impassively with a deadness in her eyes and said, "You don't understand. My life is over. I don't have anything to say to anybody." Her husband came down right away and after being informed that she tried to have him killed, he immediately posted her $75,000 bail on the spot to get her out of jail. She was never seen again, nor were her children!

She never showed up for her court date. A couple of days later, the house was empty and the children were removed from school. I would assume—and it's only an assumption—that she is either dead or living in the Middle East as a virtual slave to the husband's family.

You see it was purely a case of greed. There were so many other options available to her, but she didn't want to give up the high lifestyle that her husband's income provided. She was willing to kill the father of her children, who committed no offense against her other than—I assume—objecting to her having a boyfriend. She was willing to kill him so that she could continue to benefit from his money.

Q: What other extremes have you seen people go to in your career for the sake of money?

MATT: Well another thing I would like to mention is the guards at Cook County Jail. For people who do not have a college degree, and in some cases don't have a high school degree, they make a very good living: between $30,000 and $50,000 a year with full benefits—medical, health, retirement, that sort of thing. I have personally participated in the prosecutions of at least ten separate guards on ten separate occasions who were willing to take $50 bribes to bring cocaine and other contraband into the jail for inmates, knowing that bringing cocaine into jail carries a mandatory minimum eight-year sentence in prison. There is no possibility of probation or any other alternative sentence. A mandatory minimum, eight years! And the guards very cavalierly take the risk. One of them said on tape as he was talking to the undercover police officer, "Hey we have to be careful, a lot of guys have been getting busted for doing this." Bear in mind, at the same time, he's risking his career, all for a $50 bribe! That's just another example of sheer stupidity and greed that I've seen people act out for money.

Q: Matt, how have these experiences shaped your personal understanding of the meaning of money?

MATT: I think that the most positive thing it's done for me is to teach me how really unimportant money is. I have two small children and a wife. I often think people lose sight of the things that are truly valuable in the world. Money is only important as a means to an end: of course you must keep in mind that it can be an end itself. So you need to evaluate the end that you're going for and decide for yourself how important it really is. I think if anything, these experiences that I've mentioned have helped me become less acquisitive, because I don't like the ugliness that I see in people who are greedy.

Q: Matt, is it fair to say that most of the people that you were prosecuting were lost to the idea of money being a means and viewed it solely as an end in itself?

Matt: Yes, they were greedy. They wanted fast cars and nice clothes. They wanted the trappings of a rich person without having to do the hard work. They wanted the money without having to do what it takes to secure money legitimately.

Q: Matt, now that you are working on the other side of the table as a defender, how has that enhanced your understanding of the meaning of money?

Matt: Well, I would have to tell you that I defend criminals because it's what I do. It's where my expertise lies. I do it to make money. I know that I need the money to pay for college educations for my two children, to feed my family, and also for pleasure—like to go on vacation and that sort of thing. It's a job that I know how to do. I do it for the money!

Q: You do it for the money?

Matt: Yes, but I have a purpose for the money.

Q: You said that with such emphasis. It sounds to me like there's a feeling of reluctance or reservation about doing it. Is that correct?

Matt: I don't know if it's a strong feeling, but there's definitely a feeling of reluctance. I think in my heart I'll always be a prosecutor because I felt that somehow I was doing something good, something that needed to be done. But by the same token, I don't think that a dentist climbs in people's mouths day in and day out because he enjoys the work or gets a sense of doing some good for the world out of it. A dentist sticks his hand in people's mouths because it's a way of making a living: it's for the money.

Q: Is it difficult representing "bad guys," killers, and thieves when you identify with the "good guys"?

MATT: It's difficult, but not extremely difficult and certainly not a difficulty that I can't handle. People are entitled to good representation. And the way I justify it is that we do have the Constitution in this country and people are presumed to be innocent until proven guilty. Even if they are in fact guilty, they still have a right to effective legal representation. I know that I can provide that and I feel that I am a necessary part of the system even if the individual is, in fact, guilty of the crime he's accused of.

Q: Matt, what is the most valuable thing to you in your life and why?

MATT: My children. I don't know if I can really put it in words. All I can say is that when my three-year-old daughter climbs up in my lap at night when I'm watching TV and says, "I love you daddy," it doesn't get any better than that!

Q: In your universe of values, what would you say is the ultimate purpose of money?

MATT: I think money is convenient. It's simply a replacement of the barter system where people traded goods and services in exchange for other goods and services and it makes trade more convenient. You can carry it around in your pocket; you can transfer it by wire. And so it's simply a means of exchange. People give me money in exchange for my services. I use that same money to buy groceries. And it's simply a convenient replacement for the barter system.

Q: Was there ever a specific event with one of your clients or in your legal practice in general, where you said to yourself, "My God, now I truly understand what money is all about"?

MATT: No, I can't really say that I have because I'm not sure that I do understand money all that well.

Q: Although you've seen people go to unusually crude extremes in the search of it.

MATT: That is correct. And the thing that I learned from that has lessened the degree to which I consider money important.

Q: Do you think your father's experience with the Central Intelligence Agency in any way affected your concept or understanding of money?

MATT: I don't know that it did when I was a young child. But it did when I was a teenager and a young adult because my father was also an attorney. We both graduated from Northwestern University Law School. He never practiced law, but was offered several opportunities—which in hindsight would have made him a millionaire many times over, all of which he turned down. He served in World War II and was involved in the Cold War. He deeply believed in his heart that he was doing his country's work. He was a patriot who had conviction in what he was doing and didn't care how much he got paid. I think that was a valuable lesson for me.

Q: It was valuable because it gave you the sense that the money was not as important as deeply felt conviction?

MATT: Yeah, something like that.

Q: It sounds to me like you're still struggling with that in your own practice. You know, defending the bad guys, so to speak?

MATT: Sure, because you know, I'm no different than anybody else. I like to have nice things. I like to have a summer home and a nice boat and all of those sorts of pleasurable things. I don't know that I'll ever resolve it. I don't know that it can be resolved.

Q: As it relates to your understanding of money, what do you think is the most important thing that you learned about yourself?

MATT: I don't know that I've figured out what drives me. But I would say being rich and sort of putting on a show, keeping up with the Joneses, desiring that other people envy you for the amount of money you have, has taught me that those things are utterly unimportant. Money is important only because of what it can do for me and my family.

Q: Do you ever define yourself in terms of how much money you have?

MATT: I certainly don't define myself solely in those terms. But I would be dishonest if I said that part of the way I evaluate myself when I'm being introspective is not related to money.

Q: What do you think it is about money that hangs up so many people in our culture?

MATT: I think money may not be the best term, wealth may be a better one. We're more concerned with wealth. I do agree with some social critics who say we're becoming a TV culture. And television shows like *Dynasty* and *Dallas* offer a distorted view of American culture.

I've come in contact recently with a lot of immigrants and their perceptions of the United States have been misinformed by watching these TV shows. I prosecuted a ring of car thieves who were stealing late-model Chevy Blazers and Jeep Cherokees and sending them back to Poland where they could get large sums of money for them. These men, rather than having the work ethic that I believe they should have—which is "Thank God we're in America. I can get a job, work hard, and make something out of myself"—instead want flashy gold jewelry, nice cars, good-looking girlfriends, Rolex watches, and all of the trappings that they've come to associate with the United States. In my mind when I think of my ancestors, they came over from Ireland working hard, and being goal directed toward taking care of their families. I may be inaccurate in that, but at least that's my perception.

Q: Do you think in general that American society is more oriented toward instant gratification?

MATT: Definitely. Recently my wife and I took a vacation to Las Vegas. It was the first time we were there. First time we went anywhere without the kids.

Q: Was this a recent trip?

MATT: Two months ago. We had never been there before and thought we would enjoy it. It was the epitome of the shallow, money-grubbing, instant-gratification American culture that I am coming to despise.

We took a ride out to the desert and were just struck at the contrast between the glaring neon strip and the stillness and the solitude of the desert. It is just something that really stands out in my mind.

Q: I can just visualize the contrast between the calm and naturalness of the desert—which might serve as a metaphor for basic human values—and the glare and the glitz of money-town, which is the most extreme example of the TV culture you were speaking of.

MATT: The glassy-eyed people, three o'clock in the morning at the gambling tables, it was just pathetic. The nice thing is you can always fly out of there!

CHAPTER 5

Art Enrichment

Dorian Sylvain

Ms. Dorian Sylvain, 37, is a painter specializing in murals and public art.

Q: What is your earliest memory of money?
Dorian: I particularly recall my sophomore year of high school when my parents were in the midst of a divorce because money became a focal point. They owned a couple of properties that they had to split. My mother had been a housewife for the entire marriage and so economics suddenly became a very serious issue for her. And even though we had been raised in a pretty middle-class environment we felt the financial pressure of the separation.

I'm from a family of five. At the time, my older sister and brother were already out of the house and we younger ones ended up living with my father. My mother had to go back to school to kind of refocus her life. And so the divorce just drew our attention to certain monetary tensions I was otherwise unaware of.

Q: What was your family's attitude toward money?
Dorian: From what I experienced it was pretty casual. Casual in the sense that they did not make it an issue with us. You know,

ART ENRICHMENT

short of hearing things like, "eat all your food, there are starving children in Africa," their attitude was pretty low key. We had plenty around us. My mother was very conservative and because there were so many children she used to shop in secondhand stores. But really it never seemed like a big deal. It was just the way we grew up and we never went without.

Q: As you were growing up, did you feel it was important for you to have money?

DORIAN: You know, Bob, as I was growing up, it only was important in comparison to other people. I started to think, "Wow, they've got this and that and I don't." This was when I was a teenager when you really start paying attention to things like that.

Q: Do you remember having any particular fantasies about money?

DORIAN: I guess mostly with clothes, because I started to resent wearing hand-me-downs and shopping at Sears and Wards. I started becoming more fashion conscious and just the whole exterior type of focus started becoming more important to me. My mother thought all that was very frivolous and she would not heed my desires in that regard.

Q: How would you characterize your current experience with money?

DORIAN: I think on the most fundamental level I deal with money in a kind of casual sense in that I don't let it run me. It's not my goal in life to have a certain amount of money or to accumulate luxury items. I really believe I've always felt that money will be there and so I don't feel a pressure about it. For example, when I chose to have my first child, you know people said, "Oh my God. What are you going to do? You're such a career woman!" But I feel if I don't pressure myself I'll be all right. I have this underlying faith that I'll be provided for and that money will come and that things will work themselves out. So I guess it is just a philosophy of an "even life." I also think that because I grew up in the manner that I did, I don't have a fear of poverty. Nor do I have a need to put money first in my life.

Q: To consume?

DORIAN: Right. I think that that's one of the reasons I've been comfortable with freelancing. I know many people who have always questioned that decision and say, "God, I could never do it." They need to have a job. They need to know what kind of money they'll be making month to month.

Q: Dorian, are you saying that they need to have financial security and you don't?

DORIAN: I have long ago come to the conclusion that this whole idea of security that we're fed in contemporary American society is really not security at all. And that personally I feel very comfortable with kind of putting it on the line and having faith that things will work themselves out.

Q: Could you talk a little bit more about your idea of security? Are you saying that there's so much insecurity in life already and there's so much that is beyond our individual control that the concept of financial security is, at its essence, illusory?

DORIAN: Exactly. I think that people buy into this idea of security because they are conditioned. They are conditioned first to be consumers and second to be employees. So it comes from just the mind-set that makes our society work. You know, we need the majority of people to be of a certain frame of mind so that they fit into what the corporations need. From an early age I've always been a freelance kind of person who just found or made opportunities and that's what provides me with security, because it allows me the possibility to fulfill my personal vision. It also allows me to have flexibility in terms of my lifestyle, whereas the average person has a pretty rigid schedule because of his or her job. And so

I've always found much more advantage—not only economically, but philosophically—in being a freelancer.

Q: I find it quite refreshing the way you're using the term freelance. I have this mental image of an adventurous Dorian "Lancelot" blazing her own paths to new adventures.

DORIAN: Bob, that's really what it is like in a lot of ways. It's an interesting visual that you gave me because I have had so many opportunities to travel and to meet fascinating people in different countries and situations and it has all been so personally fulfilling. And I think it is a result of allowing that openness and that freedom in my life. In reality I could have always gotten a job, but I intentionally kept myself open. As a matter of fact, I remember when I moved back to Chicago after living in San Francisco for quite a while I was just determined not to get a job. I remember that at the time I needed the money, but I wouldn't allow myself to get locked into a nine-to-five situation. I got involved with this network of elderly women and I just started house painting, just anything to keep myself open to other opportunities with my art, and it made all the difference in the world. I mean I was able to make a few dollars. But the important point is that it kept me open.

Q: Dorian, what is the most valuable thing to you in your life and why?

DORIAN: At the risk of sounding like a cliché, as a mother I'd certainly have to say my children. A few years earlier my answer would have been very different.

Q: What would it have been then?

DORIAN: Before the children were born it would have been my painting. My artwork was the driving force at the time. And though it's still very much a part of my life, it definitely has taken a backseat to taking care of the kids. But you know I still look to my art as being a central aspect of how I live my life. And I mean that holistically in the sense that my art is a profound lifestyle choice. The implications are broader than just what it is that I create. It is also what I bring to my children: the environment that I raise them in. So now the art has taken on a new dimension in my life. For example, our kids, as young as they are, go to concerts, museums, and the theater. I remember my oldest when he was just three weeks old, I would take him to the theater with me. Now he goes to all the openings and the same with our one-and-a-half-year-old. I take them with me to work and so it exposes them to a wide variety of environments and situations that is not available to most kids. I find that to be real satisfying in comparison to the average child's experience, which is day care at a very early age. I feel that my children are just blessed with these opportunities and experiences because of my husband's and my lifestyle and careers. I think it makes them some pretty cool little kids!

Q: Dorian, what do you think is the ultimate purpose of money?

DORIAN: Bob, I look at it simply as a means of freeing myself to be able to do the things I want to do. When things are tight economically it really produces a lot of stress. When money is abundant and there is a good flow, it allows for the freedom not to worry about it.

Q: That's such a precise term in every sense in relation to money isn't it? Flow?

DORIAN: Yeah, it is. You know that's how I really look at it. It's like either there's a good flow or there's a bad flow.

Q: I was thinking it also provides for understanding flow in the psychological sense.

DORIAN: Right, it's not the flow of money for the sake of money. It's for the sake of what kind of psychological freedom money affords us as individuals and as parents. And you know my husband and I strive for money in that sense, in terms of what experiences it can provide. One of the big things around our home is art. We love to have a lot of original art. And that again is not from an economic standpoint but rather from a spiritual outlook. We believe that there is something spiritual about being in its presence. So we put a lot of money into it. We don't purchase electronic gadgets or things like that.

Q: Dorian, how has being an artist shaped or affected your personal concept of money?

DORIAN: The first thing that comes to mind is the typical philosophy of an art student: starve yourself and feed your palate. I think we really have to acknowledge that we live in a society that strongly embraces this idea of the starving artist. I cannot say that I am any longer a subscriber of that philosophy! But that was one of my early influences in the sense that the money is not important. So you paint because you love it, even if it means sacrifice. And so once I was in that mind-set I just learned to deal with my work because that was the priority. I was not the kind of adolescent that was in a quandary about which way I should go with my life. I knew when I was very young that art was what I wanted to do. And so I was on this mission from the start to become an artist. In retrospect it probably was very healthy to let go of any ideas of money and just concentrate on perfecting my talent because that is what's most important. As I became more mature I also realized that there's no reason that I have to sacrifice monetarily. A lifestyle of abundance is not contradictory to creating art!

I think it is important, however, to keep in mind that if we as a society continue to perpetuate the image and philosophy of the starving artist, it has dire implications on the value of artists. I think too often artists who are really out there, working and making things happen, find themselves in a position where they need to justify their own value both as artists and human beings.

Q: Dorian, to what extent do you think money has significantly affected the quality of your life?

Dorian: For me, money certainly has not been the driving force. However, money has provided me with a comfortable lifestyle. Also, and this may touch on the idea of the starving artist, I've always felt worthy of being paid fairly for what I do. And so I make sure as a businessperson that I'm compensated adequately. So I've always had a good flow of money as an artist. Probably more than most of my contemporaries. I've worked hard, but at the same time I feel that I deserve what I earn. So for me, money has been a provider of a very comfortable life. It's always been important to me that I live in a nice neighborhood, that I have a nice home, that I have a vehicle, and that I eat well. So when those things are taken care of, I feel very wealthy in terms of how I'm able to live. Now with children I have a new priority: saving money. But I still have a basic image of how it is that I like to live. And so money has been very useful in that regard. It has allowed me to fulfill my ambition and career choices.

Q: Why do you think Americans get so hung up about money?

Dorian: I think I touched on it earlier; because we're raised to be consumers. I think it's just very cultural. And what is most disturbing is that it goes against what is basic to our nature: the quest for satisfaction on a more spiritual level. I think that we really fall for the consumerist doctrine with all its emphasis on money. We start believing that it really means something to drive a certain kind of car and wear certain kinds of clothes. Of course you may enjoy them, but it's a matter of perspective! And I think we place far too much importance on that. I think the root of all this is the corporate structure of our society. And so "they" have got to entice us into feeling like these *things* mean something!

Q: We're always left with the message that somehow we're insufficient: that we don't measure up until we own corporations' products or use their services. You know, we either don't look right or act right or even die right until we own their insurance/plots/caskets—you name it!

DORIAN: Exactly. But once you acquire these things according to the doctrine, you're supposed to be cool. But it never works out that way!

Life is supposed to be good, but yet people find that they have emotional problems. They still may have problems with their parents or they may feel lonely or insecure. All the money in the world won't assuage those fundamental human concerns. I think that all this consumerism becomes an ugly delusion, which is psychologically destructive. I think in part that's why people fall apart around this ideology . . . why they still need to shoot up heroin and find an escape. You can have all the money in the world and great electric gadgets and still feel unhappy! The advertisers are so successful because they know how to exploit the feeling that something is always missing and no matter how much you have you will always feel incomplete and want more.

Bob, just look around. See where American society places its emphasis on what is important! Things that are really significant like developing human character and family values, we give little attention to. Consider single-parent families. What is going on in this society where people cannot hold relationships together! There again, I believe, we should as a society place profound emphasis on the importance of learning to establish and maintain meaningful long-term relationships.

I also think one of the really blatant messages that comes through loud and clear in the media and advertising is that *products* make you independent and self-sufficient. That you really don't need anyone else! You can be an island unto yourself. Look at what our youth are being fed on MTV and in music videos. Consider what they're being taught! It's pretty scary because they're not being equally exposed to values of love or of commitment to family. They're being shown sex and violence, all of which is being glorified. Girls are being told that you can be this cool superfly woman and you don't really need a man. You don't need a relationship because you are a complete package once you get your BMW and you have your wardrobe set!

Q: It's just such a distorted message, isn't it?

DORIAN: Well it's just constantly reinforced and repeated in the media that all you have to do is look a certain way, act a certain way, and hang out in the right places! It's all very empty and is not about positive human interaction. It's not about any higher way of thinking. To me it detracts from our dignity and value as human beings.

Q: Dorian, what you're saying is the media's promotion of consumerism and materialism is deeply destructive to the overall ethos of American society, is that right?

DORIAN: I really believe it is because I think that ultimately what people find is that there's still an emptiness, and unconsciously realize that all the things that are being promoted and advertised are not, in the final analysis, about anything substantial.

Q: As it relates to the whole issue of money, what is it that you learned most about yourself?

DORIAN: How should I put this? I've learned that in this society there is an abundance of resources and opportunities and that I am worthy of those things. And if I keep myself open, they will be available to me. All I have to do is concentrate on my art and bring value into my life. And to just keep on having faith. . . .

I know that I have found myself in periods when I'm really driven by the money. For example, I may be going through a tight time financially and I will find myself taking on projects just because it's paying a certain amount of money. And then what happens is that I start feeling this conflict and I ask myself, "Why are you doing this?" And I've found in my life it's not rewarding unless the project is meaningful. So I have to really keep a strong perspective of what feels good to me, what brings me satisfaction spiritually and artistically. I can't allow myself to get caught in jobs where

ART ENRICHMENT

I'm working just for the money, just for the sake of making a few dollars.

Q: So would it be fair to say, then, what you've learned is that you just have to be true to your own sense of personal values?

DORIAN: True to what it is that I want. I mean, I can't compromise my work or time just for the sake of money because ultimately, I know the money will come. You see, I've always had things around me. I think that comes from the way I was raised. I mean I know people who were raised in very tight economic conditions and they always have a certain paranoia about them about being poor. And maybe because I grew up in a middle-class family—even though I had brushes with financial stress during my parents' divorce—basically I always felt secure and provided for.

Q: You know, I think one of the things that comes through to me in almost all the interviews is that people really are very true to their personal values. We really are very consistent. In fact, it amazes me just how consistent we are! For you, value has always derived from being true to yourself and your art and your basic principles. The money has never been, as you say, the driving force or at the forefront of your experience. And for the person for whom money has been at the forefront from the beginning, nothing—it appears—is going to change that.

In many respects that's the illusion of money. People think that they can spend the first 30 or 40 years of their lives just focusing on the money and then later completely change their outlook. I think that is truly the exception.

DORIAN: Right, because the thing is that you've already established priorities and values and set yourself in motion in terms of your choices and life patterns. For me, I know, money is something that provides a lifestyle. But it's not the money itself. It's kind of like some people say "I'm going to wait to have kids until I can really afford them." Well, when the hell can you ever afford kids? I don't believe there is ever a right moment but *now* to do whatever it is that you find important. This idea that you have to achieve a certain economic plateau before you can enjoy life or before you can experience personal freedom—or that you have to put in 60-hour weeks before you can experience children—is an illusion. It's a fallacy. You just make it happen! I think, Bob, that's really what I've been saying to myself all along. It's up to me to make it happen. You know it comes to you sometimes by just not worrying about it. That is ultimate financial security.

CHAPTER 6

KISS: Keep It Simple, Stupid

Larry Rosenberg

MR. LARRY ROSENBERG, 59, is president of Lakeshore Asset Management Company. He is the former chairman of the Chicago Mercantile Exchange.

▼

Q: Larry, what is your earliest memory of money?

LARRY: I was in grade school and like a lot of kids I would work at chores and receive an allowance for it. I was pretty frugal and would save all my money. I even had a strongbox that I used to keep my money in!

Q: You had a strongbox at home?

LARRY: Absolutely. A little gray safe. I remember that I carried the key with me. It was the kind that you could break into with a bread knife if you lost the key.

Q: Did it give you a sense of security keeping your money under lock and key?

LARRY: It certainly did. I also had a savings account at the local bank, but I always liked to have some cash on me!

Q: Where did you get that attitude from?

Larry: I think it's my Eastern European heritage. It's the old shtetl mentality.

Q: Well, that gets me to my next question, Larry. What was your family's attitude toward money?

Larry: Money was to enjoy. If you did well financially you took care of the essentials, and that included social obligations such as charities and so forth. After that you just enjoy it!

Q: As you were growing up, do you remember having any particular thoughts about money?

Larry: Yes. I always wanted to have enough money to enjoy life and the things that money affords. I always wanted to provide for my family and those closest to me. I also believe strongly that when you have money, you support causes, and that brings a lot of personal pleasure and fulfillment.

Q: Larry, are you saying that as you were growing up, you thought that you'd like to be in a position to help other people with your money?

Larry: Very definitely. I think that's part of the obligation of having money. It's a responsibility to yourself and to others.

Q: Do you remember as you were growing up having any particular fantasies about money?

Larry: No, I was never really obsessed with money.

Q: Do you believe that money is either the root of all evil or the sum of all blessings?

Larry: No, I don't think it's either. You know, we can cite all kinds of examples of miserable people with a lot of money and contented people with no money. What I think is clear is that money doesn't care who owns it. I think it's what you do with it that reflects your personal character. In some respects money is like a gun. You can put a gun in one man's hand and he'll go hunting, engaging in a legal activity; and another guy is going to commit a crime and shoot someone.

Q: Larry, you're certainly someone who's had his fair share of money.

LARRY: Yes, indeed.

Q: You've owned great houses and cars and traveled all around the world.

LARRY: Airplanes, boats . . . I've been very fortunate, I've done it all.

Q: What have you learned, do you think, from your experiences with money?

LARRY: I've found that many times you become a captive of your possessions and I don't care how much money you have, money alone doesn't bring pleasure. I'm far more content today, having simplified my life, than I was with all my possessions in the past. I now do exactly what I want to do when I want to do it, and I don't feel that I'm chasing my tail!

Q: To what extent do you think as you were growing up that you measured yourself by how much money you had?

LARRY: I don't think I ever thought of it in dollars and cents terms. But when I was younger it was more of an ego thing. You look at yourself in terms of "look what I have!" Today I couldn't care less! I think the older you get, you end up with fewer but closer friends. These are far more important to me than having "zillions." I live comfortably, and truthfully, I'm very content.

Q: Do you ever think in terms of how much is enough?
LARRY: No.

Q: What would you say is most valuable to you?

Larry: My kids. I believe in family. When I grew up I was very fortunate. My dad and I were very close, although he died at an early age.

Q: How old was he?

Larry: He was 46 and I was 19 at the time. When he died he left me a good name. Hopefully, I will do the same for my three boys! And we're very close, too, and to me that's real value. To me value in one's life is being able to bring up good citizens and that's a real contribution every parent should make to society.

Q: To what extent do you think money has significantly affected the quality of your life?

Larry: It's kind of funny when you think about it. I've had a lot of pleasure out of money, but some of the major aggravations in my life have been because of money—that whole treadmill we get on, you know, chasing our tail for the sake of the almighty dollar! It has been great, but it's been a two-edged sword.

Q: Larry, what do you think is the ultimate purpose of money?

Larry: Money is a necessary commodity. Its purpose is to provide things for your family, for yourself, and to help others. It is to be enjoyed. And let me underscore something that I said before because it is something I truly believe in: If you're fortunate enough to have money, it is an obligation to make some contribution back to society.

Q: Larry, let me ask you another question. You're currently president of an asset management company, managing tens of millions of dollars. You were formerly chairman of an exchange that specializes in trading money. You've met with important political and financial people throughout your career. As you consider all your experiences and look around at today's culture, why do you think people get so hung up about money?

Larry: My read, and I think I have earned an opinion because I spent personal time on the treadmill, is that the quest for money

KISS: KEEP IT SIMPLE, STUPID

is no different than chasing your tail! If I buy a 30-foot boat, then you get a 40-foot boat, so I'll have to buy a 60-foot boat. Whatever! It's always bigger, faster. You own a three-car garage. OK. When I build my house, I'll have a four-car garage. You're never happy with what you have!

Q: I saw an article in the *New York Times* today. It was talking about the biggest status symbol now among the young successful New York stock brokers is luxury watches that cost $100,000 plus.

LARRY: In the meantime, if you buy a Casio, it keeps better time!

Q: But, you know, Larry, it is indicative of how crazy these things get.

LARRY: Been there and done that! Bob, I had a watch that sold at auction for $150,000. It was a Patek Phillipe Calender Chronograph. You're looking at a guy who used to own five cars. I've had Ferraris, Porsches. Anything with wheels that was fast and expensive, I've owned it! And believe me when I tell you I'm much happier now that I don't own a car. I live downtown. I take taxis to and from work and it's just fine. As I said earlier, you become a captive of your possessions. You truly do and I wanted out!

It's an old hackneyed expression, but it's true. Money does not buy happiness. Buying bigger and faster cars will not improve your life!

Q: What will?

LARRY: For me that's real easy! I'm married to a wonderful person. My kids are grown, but we see a lot of each other. I love to travel. Going out for a fine meal with good friends, simple stuff!

Q: Larry, are you saying that as you got older you realized that the relationships that you formed with friends have become more important.

LARRY: Exactly. Relationships are the whole thing. I mean, if you don't have meaningful relationships in your life, where is the wealth? The absence of relationships is in my opinion the worst kind of poverty.

Q: Larry, as it relates to your understanding of money and values, what do you think is the most important thing that you've learned about yourself?

LARRY: That money really doesn't make you happy. You have to find happiness elsewhere. I mean, money can be used for wonderful purposes, but just acquiring things, being acquisitive is a waste of time. I see people in my business—I'm talking about people in their 80s, even, with tens of millions of dollars—where more money clearly has no significance and they're still after more. They're still in the game, and they haven't stopped to smell the roses. They're still just passing by.

Q: But you have made a conscious effort in your life to change?

LARRY: Yes I have. I've really thought a lot about it, and I said, my God, what really is important?

Q: And what you have done basically is simplify your lifestyle. Is that correct?

LARRY: Yes. Maybe to an extreme.

Q: Can you give me an example?

LARRY: Well, as I said before, I sold all my cars and I found it quite liberating. Actually, it is very interesting. It was almost as if I felt more secure after I got rid of stuff than I ever felt before. It was really enlightening.

Q: Larry, it's ironic that the security you were looking for came from getting rid of stuff, rather than acquiring it.

LARRY: It's incredible, but it's absolutely true. Boats, cars, planes, Rolexes . . . all the things I owned. I don't have any of them anymore.

Q: You don't have to.

LARRY: Excuse me?

Q: I said, you don't have to. You don't need them!

LARRY: Yes. I heard you the first time. I was just letting it register. I don't think I've ever been this content before.

CHAPTER 7

All the President's Men

Rich Buendorf

MR. RICH BUENDORF, 31, was a Secret Service agent from 1989 to 1995. He was assigned to President Bill Clinton. He now develops properties in the inner city of Chicago.

▼

Q: Rich, what is your earliest memory of money?
RICH: I was about seven and my friends and I were trying to build a tree fort. I had to come up with money to buy the lumber.

Q: For the tree fort?
RICH: Yes, this was in Minneapolis.

Q: Did you come up with the money?
RICH: Yeah, we actually put a carnival together for all the neighbors and raised quite a bit of money.

Q: So you were enterprising.
RICH: It turned out pretty good. I think we made about $48, and we built the fort.

Q: What did you learn from that experience about money?
RICH: It gave me an opportunity to get the things that I wanted. From that age on I learned that the harder I work at something, the

better are my chances of accomplishing my goals and being successful.

Q: What was your family's attitude toward money when you were growing up?

RICH: Well, initially we were poor. My father was a teacher and he had to raise three kids. We weren't really dinging the bell. Later he went on to an executive position, and we started to belong to the country club and have, you know, a Cadillac and a summer home and things like that. I remember that when we were at the country club I was always made to feel that we didn't come from old money. My mom wasn't quite fully accepted as one of the people in the country club. So we didn't quite fit in, even though we had the money to be there.

Q: As you were growing up, what were your thoughts about money?

RICH: I think it often made me feel like I didn't belong. If you didn't have the right clothing or you didn't live in a certain neighborhood, you weren't included in the group.

Q: So you felt as though you were excluded from things?
RICH: Exactly.

Q: Did you believe money was something that you wanted or needed to allow you to belong?

RICH: I always felt that it was something I needed to allow me to have the freedom to do the things that I wanted. I never had a desire to have a lot of materialistic things, because I was able to observe how it seemed to make other people greedy.

Q: Rich, you were a Secret Service agent for six years. You were assigned to President Clinton when he was running for office. In what way do you think that experience has either shaped or affected your concept of money?

Rich: Bob, that's a great question, because when President Clinton was first running for office, he had about as much of a chance of winning as I did. George Bush, it was thought, was definitely going to be reelected. There was a feeling that this candidate who we were guarding was a loser. I don't mean that personally I felt he was a loser, it was just the prevailing attitude in the Democratic Party and among Americans in general.

Q: Was that the attitude of the Secret Service agents?

Rich: No, not really. However, I guess most agents felt like Paul Tsongas was probably going to be picked on the Democratic side, and Bush was actually going to win the election. So initially you really didn't see a lot of people palling around with Clinton. Interestingly, Clinton himself never once thought he wasn't going to win. It was an exciting time and Clinton's enthusiasm was really something. What is most interesting is that when the polls turned around in August of 1992, and it looked like Clinton was the frontrunner, things really changed. Man, did people start sucking up! All of a sudden everybody was Bill's best buddy. People and corporate sponsors with money started coming out of the woodwork looking to position themselves.

Q: So you actually saw the moneyed people coming up to him?

Rich: Yeah, you saw the change in attitude. All of a sudden people began thinking this guy might have some power and it was a whole new ball game.

Q: Do you remember what your perception was at the time?

Rich: It was disenchanting for me, because I began to realize the very nature of the position of president requires that he has to represent the people who are helping him get elected. And unfortunately, that's not all the American people; a lot of it is the interest groups. I could see them firsthand slowly carve away at the principles that Clinton stood for. A candidate may have a strong personal feeling . . . But look at President Bush, for example, who was very much pro abortion and adopted a stance as an antiabortion candidate. So, it was disappointing, because I wanted to see somebody in office who had an independent character and who would represent all of the people. And instead, what happened is you got a candidate who was peeled back to represent a select group of vested individuals.

Q: Rich, you observed this happening? You saw the financial interests coming forward, so that in your opinion Clinton's speeches started getting pared down to serve them.

RICH: Well, right, but this happened on both sides—it's not Democrat or Republican. Unfortunately it's American politics. You also see volunteers or staffers working on the president's campaign who have the money to take off a year to be able to wear the right suit or outfit that's presentable. People without money don't have the time or funds to do that. And it's all done for the payoff that comes with victory. I've seen campaign workers who as a result of their having money were able to spend a lot of time with the candidate or get into his good graces. And I also witnessed the candidate making accommodations in his point of view based on the people who were willing to support his candidacy.

Q: So how did this experience affect your personal concept of value and money?

RICH: You know, the best thing about being an agent in the Secret Service is that you can be around this environment and then see it from the outside like a fishbowl. When you go back to your local neighborhood you're nobody. I mean, you're just another person. And because of that, you're able to listen to what is the unsolicited response of the American public. You get to hear what regular people's gripes are, not a polished version to make it appear better to the president in order to get into his good graces.

Q: Rich, what stands out in your mind about your experience with President Clinton?

RICH: I'm always amazed how people react to someone of celebrity status. How people will stand around for hours just to see somebody famous. And it leads me to believe that people are afraid to realize that we're all the same. People crack up almost in disbelief when I tell them the president passes gas when he goes jogging. People are amazed at that, and I go, "Why?" You know, this is just a normal person. I find it disappointing when I see so many people act as if they're blind, acting as though they aren't capable when they really are. Clinton would hold a baby and mothers would cry. You know, people would pass out in line as soon as he shook their hand. The agents are actually trained to respond to when a person gets so nervous shaking the president's hand that he doesn't let go. We practice release techniques for those situations. You know, it's not because they're trying to hurt the president, they're just so excited that they finally got to meet him. I think that what I found to be great about the job was that I learned that the president really is just another person with a big job.

Q: Rich, there's so much talk now about the president's character that I think I would be remiss if I didn't ask you this question. Given your observations about the role of money in the campaign coupled with the fact that you actually spent a lot of time during the campaign speaking alone with the president, from your viewpoint what kind of man is Bill Clinton and how has this experience shaped your own sense of personal value?

RICH: My personal observation is that the presidency seems like a very lonely position. I watched Bill Clinton run for the office of president and I sensed a certain insecurity because everybody tries to be your friend. I think he really struggled as do most people at that level with who should be trusted. What I learned from that experience was you have to judge what people are willing to do for somebody other than themselves. You have to be able to determine if they're willing to give rather than to take.

Q: Rich, let's pursue the issues of character and personal values. You made a career change in 1995 that certainly does not appear to be the next logical step from being a Secret Service agent. You've established your own foundation and you buy properties in the inner city—Englewood is one of the most deprived areas in the country. You work with local people and help develop their housing. Can you talk a little bit about that?

RICH: Prior to getting a job with the Secret Service, I was assistant city manager for St. Anthony, Minnesota. Taking into consideration that I was a political science major in college and had worked for the president, doing what I'm doing now really is not all that inconsistent.

As a Secret Service agent, I often got a chance to go into neighborhoods and see how normal American people, white and black, lived their lives. I would see people heating their houses with all the burners going on the stove. I'd see little kids running around unattended. And I'd ask questions about it. I think a lot of people in the law enforcement community are kind of callous to the people in these neighborhoods. They feel like they're all the same. In reality, they are just people who are poor. The kind of people who keep their milk cold on the back porch because that's all they have. And what they want in actuality is to be like you and me or the next guy who can take a trip with his kids to Disney World. What I learned was a lot of people have desire but unfortunately no direction. So even though they may have opportunity in the world, when they do, they don't know where to begin to establish and then meet meaningful goals. I started in a very simple way, creating a quality of life for people, which creates hope. I believe giving people a good place to live enables them to look at their life differently. And then I realized that it was an investment opportunity as well.

A house built in Lincoln Park or on the South Side of Chicago is really the same if you don't have any renters in it. It's valueless. So your investment is only as good as the people who are in it. And in my case, I wanted to strengthen my tenants and at the same time strengthen my investment. So I would not only give them a high quality of life, but we started creating a job placement program and a résumé service. We even started to teach trade skills. And all of a sudden, not only do they have a good place to live, but they have hope that they now have a job. You know it also breaks down psychological barriers. If you give people hope, they confide in you. Someone will turn to you if you allow them not to feel embarrassed and say, "Hey, I'm 42 years old. I've never read before" or "I don't have a birth certificate." We have one kid in our mentorship program who's 13 years old and he was unbelievably embarrassed because he never had a father. His father was killed in a drug trade. He was embarrassed to tell anybody—because he never had a man around—that one of his testicles had never dropped. I mean, that's the kind of stuff that once you break down psychological barriers people are willing to come out with. And you can see their humanity. People don't want handouts!

Q: Yes, they want hope and respect!

RICH: Exactly. And they also want direction and purpose. You know, Bob, I've worked around the rich and famous. I've seen how the princes of various oil countries spend money. That kind of wealth is just numbing. They would just drop $20,000 gifts like it was nothing. I've seen that and I didn't feel comfortable with it. In contrast, on the South Side I'll go visit somebody who's homeless. He may have only a cup of soup, but he's willing to share half of everything he owns with me. It's very humbling, and it makes me feel very welcome. In Washington, you have to play politics. You've got to know people, and you've got to play by their rules. You're a somebody only because of your material wealth or what you're perceived to be able to do for someone! In Washington, if you say "left," by the time you're done, everyone will know what you really meant was "right" anyway.

Q: Rich, what do you think is the ultimate purpose of money?

Rich: I think the ultimate purpose of money is freedom. It allows you the freedom to choose. I think that somewhere along the line we've lost that value. Today people want to horde money. I think as soon as a society starts hoarding money and individuals say, "It's mine, I don't want to share it," that's the beginning of a culture's demise.

Q: Is it one of your goals to allow people on the South Side to have more opportunities to choose from? Is that part of it?

Rich: Very much so. I told everybody, the day I start making $2, I make room for them to make $1. As soon as I make $4, I make that much more room for more people to make $2 and the next group to make $1. And you know, the whole idea is community growth, so that everybody has opportunity.

Q: Where did you learn that value system?

Rich: Somebody else recently asked me, "Why do you do this?" I don't know. It must have come from my parents. My dad fought in Korea. He worked hard and had good values. My mom was a dedicated mother who used to say to all of us when we were kids that no one person is more important than the next, the group is only as strong as the weakest link. I remember her asking us as children, "What is the point of moving quickly ahead when we should be stopping to help somebody else catch up?"

Q: Why do you think people get so hung up about money?

Rich: I really think it comes down to insecurity. Once you get into a comfort zone, you don't like to get out of it. And the more you stay in it, the easier it becomes. I'm surprised when I go down to the South Side how afraid of whites people are. And the opposite is true about blacks in Lincoln Park, which is almost all white. Here my neighbors are surprised that I go down to the South Side. It's old habits, tired thought patterns, and insecurity. I think it's the same thing with money.

Q: Rich, as it relates to your understanding of money, what do you think is the most important thing that you learned about yourself?

RICH: That no matter how well intentioned you are and how much you're willing to trust someone or some group, there will be someone coming along to con you, to question your motives, or to take your money. And you have to fight from becoming bitter, because that's the very nature of people. You want to pull back and quit helping others. But you must remember the overriding goal. So you've got to just keep doing what you think is right, getting out there, and sometimes getting bit.

From my perspective, the objective is to be able to provide the opportunity for others to succeed. It may sound corny, but it is amazing to watch the transformations I've observed on a personal level.

There's this guy, he goes by the name "D"—just the letter "D." I know his real name, but he doesn't like people to know. When we met him, he was living in an abandoned building, where he collected his drinking water from rusty pipes. He'd defecate on a piece of paper and take it out to the garbage when he was done. When I purchased the building, he was squatting in, he thought we were just going to put him out on the street. Now that would be normal. But to really build, you have to try to build the character of the people in a community. So we took "D" in. We gave him a small responsibility—something we knew he couldn't fail at. And he did it. I said, "I want you to call me when you're done," and he called. We have an 800 number just for the people who don't have their own phones. As time passed, we gave "D" more responsibility and eventually moved him into a two-bedroom apartment. Then we got him a refrigerator, a stove, a kitchen table and chairs, and a bed. Before we knew it, "D" had a furnished apartment, and he was managing the four-unit building that he lived in. His job was secured. He helped keep the gangbangers away. He took pride in his building. He kept the drug pushers away and maintained the property because he believed it was his own. Today "D" manages three of our buildings. He collects the rent and shows the new apartments. You see, Bob, what I'm trying to accomplish is helping all the "Ds" build confidence in who they are as people.

I think what I learned the most from what I'm doing is just so basic: treat people the way you want to be treated. Just believe that there are more good people than bad people. And be willing to take the risk that somebody might steal from you, that they may try to con you, but even so keep believing that there's that one person like "D" that you can help. The loyalty and the trust just keeps growing. If you help people in this way, they will do anything for you.

Q: Sounds like you're trying to build your own Secret Service.
RICH: I never thought of it that way!

CHAPTER 8

Jazz Warrior

Kahil El'Zabar

MR. KAHIL EL'ZABAR, 43, is an internationally acclaimed jazz musician. He is also an arts activist and educator.

Q: What is your earliest memory of money?
KAHIL: Probably buying myself ice cream. Understanding that currency could purchase the things that I wanted. My family was lower middle class but lived in an upper-middle-class area, which meant they were very resourceful.

Q: What do you mean?
KAHIL: Well, they married when they were 16 and 19 years old. Without Mom working outside the home they were able to buy a house while they were in their early 20s, which meant that they really had to be resourceful. You know they didn't go to restaurants and spend their money foolishly. They weren't raised to spend their money in a certain kind of way.

Q: They weren't extravagant?
KAHIL: Exactly. They saw money as something they desired but also respected. They associated money with status, but it was certainly something that they didn't have a lot of experience with. For

example, both my parents believed a lot in quality and they found unique ways to stretch their money. I mean I always wore nice clothes but they were usually secondhand. There was a store called Repeat Petite in the Gold Coast area. We would drive up from the South Side to get things there. They were inexpensive, but it was all about quality. It was just something natural to both of them. The way they kept our home and the way they presented themselves was all about quality. So Bob, I think it established an important perspective for me when I was growing up. That the key was not so much the money as the overriding quality of things.

Q: So the emphasis was not on monetary value?

KAHIL: Right. Quality of engagement, quality of conversation, quality of preparing food, and quality of self-presentation—those were the things that counted.

You know from the time I was nine or ten years old I looked at money as something that could acquire things. But money couldn't make a joke!

Q: Couldn't make a joke?

KAHIL: Right. I mean, my father was really good at that. We always had dinner together and he would hold court. He would judge us to see if we could exemplify his style and appreciation of quality. And that had to do with wit, intellect, intuition, and emotion. So those were the things that became dominant in terms of what I valued.

Q: So for you, Kahil, would it be fair to say money has not been a driving force?

KAHIL: For me, the quest has been more of a search for energy than to secure material things, even though the material is attractive. I think in truth my mother was probably more enamored by the idea of acquiring money even though we never really were able to. My father, on the other hand, was just always comfortable with how people engaged one another and how they formed relationships and things like that.

Q: Your mother tried to acquire money?

KAHIL: Status and the money associated with that. But you know, I saw in her a certain frustration that she wasn't able to achieve the level that she wanted. On the other hand, my father was just always really comfortable in all kinds of settings and situations. It was something that I aspired to at an early age. I wanted to find that same center for myself. But again, for me, the quest has always been more about energy than acquiring the material. Securing the energy was the way to move closer to the objectives you value in your life.

Q: Kahil, how would you sum up your feeling about money?

KAHIL: I look at money as illusive conjecture.

Q: How do you mean that?

KAHIL: Money is always illusive and seems to be subject to a variety of faulty opinions of what has true value. All of which, in fact, may have little or no value for me!

Q: How would you characterize your current relationship with money?

KAHIL: I'm not the most frugal person.

Q: I can see that by the way you're dressed. You're all in suede and leather.

KAHIL: OK. But the point I want to make is the reality that money is a means of exchange in the world that we exist in. However, it is not for me an inspiring force. I'm not inspired by money and it does not motivate my thoughts and actions.

Q: What does inspire you?

KAHIL: Content in humanity inspires me: pursuit of excellence and positive energy. I'm inspired by the music of Thelonius Monk as well as that of Vladimir Horowitz. I'm equally inspired by the architecture of Frank Lloyd Wright as I am by a good parent or person who demonstrates trust. I'm inspired by friendship and all the qualities that represent the most positive aspects of human beings. I'm also inspired and value the physical and athletic intensity of Michael Jordan as much as the musical excellence of Miles Davis or the tenacity of Thurgood Marshall's commitment and fight for civil rights.

Q: Kahil, you are speaking of the intellectual and emotional commitment to some positive purpose. Is that correct?

KAHIL: Right. And I believe deeply that any situation—no matter how extreme—presents positive and creative possibilities in terms of individual choice. The intensity and commitment of our choices is what allows us to exploit creative resources and come up with solutions.

Q: Let's talk a little bit how you made your choice to become a musician.

KAHIL: When I was growing up, the musician was a noble figure in my community. Just think about the names: Duke Ellington, Count Basie, even Earl "Fatha" Hines. These individuals had charisma. They had style. They had a purpose in the community and they helped people elevate their essence. They were about quality that would rub off just through listening to them or seeing them perform. From the very beginning I was attracted to the style.

Q: The style meaning the lifestyle of the musician?

KAHIL: The lifestyle and the quality of being a musician. There was a pursuit of excellence and it was so serious, Bob! I mean you didn't play with it! Just the idea of becoming a John Coltrane, a Miles Davis, a Duke Ellington, or a Charlie Parker. There actually was nothing higher for me in the community.

Q: Was your father a musician?

KAHIL: No. He was a policeman. He was a sergeant on the Chicago police force. He played music, but never professionally. My mother's brother was a professional musician who had played with Charlie Parker and Fats Waller. And so I was around musicians all my life. Neither of my brothers, though, were attracted to it at all. One is in business and the other is a biochemist.

Q: Kahil, what would you say is the ultimate purpose of money?

KAHIL: Again Bob, I believe money is something to be used in progressive and productive ways that will ultimately enhance humanity. Look around us! Just consider for a moment the conspicuous consumption and materialism of contemporary America. It is a society that doesn't promote thinking. And the more the consumerism is intensified, the worse the result of nullifying individual thought.

Q: Do you think it's a case of lack of thinking or one of insecurity?

KAHIL: I would say that the insecurity is just the reaction. The cause is that there is an enormous investment in the society to influence public opinion toward mediocrity.

Q: What have you done personally to counteract this?

KAHIL: Well, I'm pretty active on associated fronts. I've been on the national task force for Arts Presenting in Education that explores the many overt and implied values inherent in art and their impact on the educational system at all levels from kindergarten through higher education. For many years I was the chairman of a music organization called the Association for the Advancement of Creative Musicians or AACM. And within that organization, we explored many of the values associated with the jazz lifestyle and thought about ways to reverse some of the negative values.

Q: You mean like drugs?

Kahil: Drugs, irresponsibility as far as taking care of your children . . . learning to take your career in your own hands and not being subjugated to the music industry. We have been able to achieve significant results just by engaging one another in our organization.

Q: Could you talk a little about how you strive to get your values across in your music?

Kahil: Well it comes back to naïveté with confidence. I'd rather not know how I'm doing it than just know it's happening, because once I know it then my pursuit changes.

Q: Well, it's like the Zen thing—that sounds like something George Bush would say!

Kahil: Right. But the investigation of my music and its impact still creates excitement in me.

Q: Are you saying that the musical process itself is an unfolding of your values?

Kahil: Right. Bob, it's like the jazz club that I own. Its name is Rituals. And it is also the name of my band. You see, I value rituals of all kinds from all cultures. They are a form of substantive engagement that responds to one's high ideals for humanity, its potential and its positive cultural impact.

Q: Kahil, as you reflect on the whole issue of wealth and values, what do you think you learned most about yourself?

Kahil: That a warrior is much more about healing and protecting than confronting and attacking.

Q: Do you see yourself as a warrior?
Kahil: Yeah!

Q: A musical warrior?
Kahil: Sure. A musical warrior, a creative warrior, a warrior against mediocrity.

Q: More in the sense of a samurai or a medieval knight; a spiritual battler against the readily accepted status quo!

KAHIL: Exactly. I see myself more as a cultural or intellectual warrior who feels a responsibility to support institutions and individuals that believe in free thought. And that's really the main thing. The music is just one aspect of that belief and value system. I believe in the family and our connectiveness with other positive and loving individuals. Also people who are willing to react against the mediocrity of popular media. We are not clueless. We are not without resources. Our ideals have a place in society and they shouldn't be confused with the plagiarized realities that we call contemporary American life.

Q: So what you really learned about yourself is that your life develops value by concentrating on values. Is that right?

KAHIL: Yeah. I like the way you put that!

CHAPTER 9

Until Death Us Do Part

Grant Jones

MR. GRANT JONES (pseudonym), 59, is a professional commodity trader and racehorse owner. He is one of the largest and most successful commodity traders in the country. He resides in New York City and Los Angeles.

Q: What is your earliest memory of money?
GRANT: Growing up and not having any.

Q: Do you remember that you had less than your friends, is that it?
GRANT: No. It's a memory of having to work if I wanted to have any money to buy something that I wanted. But, you know, when I was growing up I didn't think about money. I was more concerned with girls and sports and wasn't worried about other stuff.

Q: So you didn't really think about money that much?
GRANT: No.

Q: What was your family's attitude toward money?
GRANT: Well, in my recollection, the only arguments my mother and father ever had were about money. Not having any,

spending too much, whatever. They weren't really violent arguments . . . we lived in a very modest apartment and I shared a room with my sister. But I also don't remember ever being deprived of anything.

Q: Do you remember money being discussed in your home?
GRANT: No.

Q: Did your parents speak with you about money?
GRANT: Only if I wanted to purchase something, then I had to go to work. They really didn't give me money. It was just understood that if I wanted something I'd have to go out and earn it.

Q: What sort of jobs did you have?
GRANT: I always worked. I worked in a supermarket in junior high school and in the summer I worked as a waiter in a camp or a hotel. I worked for four years in a Chinese restaurant for tips delivering food. That was a very lucrative job! And while I was at college I worked afternoons in an insurance broker's office in the financial district making deliveries. I learned from a young age that I'd have to work hard in order to have money. You see my parents weren't rich and so it just became my responsibility to provide for myself. I'm sure they would have given me money if they had had it.

Q: So, what you got out of that experience was that you just had to make your own way. Is that correct?
GRANT: Right.

Q: Do you remember having any particular thoughts or fantasies about money?
GRANT: No. My adolescent fantasies were mostly sexual.

Q: That's a different book! Grant, you've come a long way from working for tips in a Chinese restaurant. Could you talk a little about how you got started in the business and how you built your fortune?

GRANT: I started as an analyst, writing a market letter for a major brokerage firm. And then I had customers and built a brokerage business within a large brokerage firm and then traded for myself. In the mid-1970s I started my own company. I started out making $300 dollars a week, going to a $100,000 and then $300,000 and then even more as my share of the brokerage increased. It was a real shock!

Q: It was a shock to you that you could make so much money?

GRANT: Right. There were limits then on what the government insured in your bank accounts. I mean, I had to have a bank account at every bank in the city in my own name, my wife's name, etc. I had to make arrangements so all this money would be insured. I used to have stacks of bank books.

Q: Grant, although today it doesn't have the same significance, crossing the million-dollar mark in annual income is still considered a major threshold. What was it like the first time for you?

GRANT: Well I was so busy I don't know whether I really thought about it. I lived in the same apartment and we didn't move to a different place until much later. It really was no big deal. My big thrill was buying an Oldsmobile instead of driving a Ford. I thought that was really something!

Q: Are you saying that when you actually started making larger sums of money, it didn't significantly affect your lifestyle?

GRANT: Yes. I saved most of the money and I really didn't know what to spend it on. I mean, I never had more than one or two suits or a sports jacket and I was too busy with my business and helping my wife to raise two kids.

Q: As you know all too well, there are many traders—perhaps the majority of traders—who make big money only to lose most or all of it in the markets or through extravagant lifestyles later on. What is your response to that?

Grant: Well, I would say that most people who I knew at the time who were also making a lot of money in the 1970s and 1980s lived as though the money was going to last forever. They thought that every year was going to be a fantastic year. And a lot of these traders bought huge homes, Rolls Royces, and jewelry and subsequently didn't have any money left. I know a few who, sadly, even committed suicide. Others are living much more modestly today. Personally I just never entered into that mind-set of spending up to the last nickel I earned. I just didn't have that kind of psychological outlook.

Q: What do you think gave you that perspective? Was it your early childhood experiences with money?

Grant: More maturity, the way I was brought up, probably the way my wife was brought up. And just good common sense, believing that the good times couldn't last forever. There is also an additional point. I was making so much that I couldn't possibly, in my own psyche, spend the amount of money I was making. It was in a way all too unreal!

Q: Grant, what does money mean to you?

Grant: To me, money means only two things. First, it means the quality of how you can live and second it provides the security of knowing that you can live in this way until you die. You can be shielded from any catastrophe such as illness, or something like that. Other than that, it doesn't mean a damn thing. You're not going to take it with you. You can't pack your valises with cash. Leaving my money to my children never was a primary goal, although I'm going to do it. But certainly spending has no high priority. The ideal goal for me would be to live a long, healthy, and active life, doing as many of the things that I want to do every year and end up at age 95 with zero.

Q: Do you think money has made you a happier person?

GRANT: Yes. Definitely. If I had never made money, I think I would still be a happy person. But I don't think that I would be strong enough to handle having made money and then losing it. I think that is a much harder thing for someone to handle. Much harder than not having made the money in the first place. I know that would have caused me a lot of psychological problems. But it's definitely made me a happier, more secure person.

Q: Do you think a lot about money?

GRANT: I probably do think about it. I don't think about how much I have. But I do think about it!

Q: Well, you know what Bunker Hunt said?
GRANT: What?

Q: "If you know how much you have, you don't have much!"
GRANT: Well there's always somebody richer than you and that never bothered me.

Q: How has being a professional speculator affected your own personal concept of money?

GRANT: Well, I certainly think that having seen a lot of people fall by the wayside, make and lose their fortunes and not being able to come back, others committing suicide has made me a lot more cautious in the things that I do.

Q: Can you think of an important experience or event in your life where you felt that you gained a deeper understanding of the real value of money?

GRANT: October 1987 in the stock market crash. I lost a million dollars screwing around in the S&P market. It's a market I usually don't even trade. I found that to be a very humbling experience!

Q: What did you learn from that experience?

GRANT: Keep away from things that you don't understand. If it looks too good to eat, it usually is!

Q: But that event didn't significantly affect your net worth, did it?

GRANT: No. But it affected my psyche. It wasn't the money. It was the meaning of the money. How could I do something so dumb!

Q: Why do you think we all get so hung up about money?

GRANT: The materialism in our society is obviously excessive. The Europeans work to live, Americans live to work! I prefer working to live. I think in general there's much too much emphasis in our culture on money. I'm a capitalist but not everything can be reduced to dollars and cents. And I think that in today's society everything is reduced to dollars and cents. I don't see anything wrong with materialism. But I would say that materialism carried to the nth degree is no good. I don't see anything wrong with socialism, but socialism carried to the nth degree is no good.

Q: I remember having a professor at Columbia who defined the difference between capitalism and socialism. He said capitalism is an economic system in which man exploits man. In socialism, it's just the other way around! So I think you're making the same point. As it relates to your understanding of money, what do you think is the most important thing that you learned about yourself?

GRANT: I think that in many ways I'm like most people. I want the same things as everybody else wants and money is the way to get things. Money is also the way you get security. I don't think I'm very different from most people in that regard. I think the only thing that is different is that I don't compare myself to other people. I don't care how much somebody else has. I never did.

Q: What do you think is most valuable to you in your life?

GRANT: That's a very difficult question to answer. One goes through life every day not thinking about what is the most valuable thing in one's life. I would say that the two things that helped me the most are my parents and getting a good education. My parents gave me the values and the good education gave me the basis for whatever followed. But I would say that meeting my wife and having two kids are the most valuable experiences in my life. That and being in good health.

Q: And that's where you continue to derive your value in life?

GRANT: Yes. I don't know whether all my values are the best values. We're only talking about money. I mean, I'm not a perfect person.

Q: That's OK, Grant, because nobody else in this book is perfect. So you're in the right company.

GRANT: You know, Bob, it's hard to count money as the most valued thing in one's life. It's basically just a means to an end. You can't take it with you so you better enjoy it while you can. However, I would think the worst thing in the world would be to die and have my wife spend it on her next husband. That is the truth! Wouldn't that be a shame! I would think that would be the biggest disappointment in anybody's life: for a successful person to make a lot of money, die, and have his wife fritter it away on her next man.

Q: Is that something that you really think about?

GRANT: No, but I just thought about it. I mean, I'm sure I've thought about it before but I don't think about it all the time.

Q: But that would bother you?

GRANT: Well, the dying part wouldn't bother me and having my wife have the money wouldn't bother me if she spent it on herself and our children. I would think if somebody took advantage of her and took that money away from her, that would bother me.

Q: I can't imagine that anybody would be able to take advantage of your wife, having been married to you for so long!

GRANT: You don't know what love can do! I mean, it can do strange things, especially to people in love for the second time. Human beings are very strange creatures!

CHAPTER 10

Rock and Salvation

Donna Hughes

MS. DONNA HUGHES, 37, is an office manager who works for a company that specializes in trading and hedging in the livestock markets.

Q: Donna, what is your earliest memory of money?

DONNA: Probably my piggy bank; getting change from parents or birthday money and putting it in my piggy bank. I was always told to save it, but I always wanted to spend it.

Q: Sounds familiar.

DONNA: So I was always searching for what I could spend my money on.

Q: Has that changed over the years?

DONNA: Yes, dramatically!

Q: What was your family's attitude toward money?

DONNA: We were middle class. My father worked two jobs so my mom could stay home with four kids. My dad was very conservative in his spending, although I remember him needing to have a new car every two years!

Q: As you were growing up, what were your thoughts about money?

DONNA: I remember always wanting to be able to work so that I could have my own money.

Q: Did you feel then that it was important for you to have your own money?

DONNA: Yes. Because then you wouldn't have to go to your parents. It was a way to be independent.

Q: Did you have any particular fantasies about money?

DONNA: I thought a lot about going on trips, traveling to far-off places. I was raised in a small town and I always dreamed about venturing out.

Q: Was there a particular place to which you wanted to travel?

DONNA: Hawaii.

Q: Why there?

DONNA: Just because I had never been there before and it was exotic.

Q: Island paradise?

DONNA: Exactly.

Q: How would you characterize your current relationship with money?

DONNA: Well, my philosophy today is that you can't have two masters so I choose not to have money as my master.

Q: What's the second one?

DONNA: The first one! God is my master.

Q: Your feeling about God has affected your relationship with money?

DONNA: Yes.

Q: Donna, could you talk about the role religion exercises in your life?

DONNA: Religion plays a central role in my life. I was raised Catholic and when I was younger I'd go to church pretty regularly, but really I didn't develop a strong spiritual relationship or understand the meaning of faith until fairly recently. It has just been for the last couple of years. Actually, it was all because of money that I was given the opportunity to strengthen my faith in God.

Q: Could you explain?

DONNA: I had just gone through a divorce and my financial situation was troubled. My state of financial well-being was always based on two incomes. After the divorce I was down to one income and I basically felt as though I was a prisoner to the things that I had accumulated. And no matter what I did to try to alleviate the monetary stress I was feeling, I experienced powerlessness to do anything about it. I know now that it was because of God's will. He pointed out to me the problem and showed me a way to resolve my dilemma with money.

Q: Donna, in your first marriage, was money a source of tension?

DONNA: Yes. Things were not perfect in the marriage to begin with and in an attempt to compensate for that I tried to make everything external appear perfect. And I thought the way to do that was to buy the things that would make it appear to be that way. I would dress my son in only the best clothes. . . . I was more concerned with appearance than reality. My faith in God has given me balance and has transformed my attitudes about money and material things.

Q: How would you characterize your current relationship with money?

DONNA: It's much more mature. It is also more conservative. Today no matter how much money I earned I would not want to go out and buy the bigger house or buy an expensive car. If I did buy a car it would be for reasons of safety and practicality; things like that.

Q: Whereas before you were buying a car . . .
DONNA: Because it was a hot car!

Q: In general, you were just more interested in extravagant things?
DONNA: Right.

Q: Donna, you work in a highly monied field. Day in and day out you're interacting with individuals who are hugely successful financially. To what extent has this experience affected your personal view of money?
DONNA: I think it was very difficult in the beginning. It was truly hard for me until I gained a more mature understanding of money. I came into this business when I was still very young. I came into contact with people who drove very expensive cars and lived in palatial homes. They took big trips. The money was just spent all over the place. And a $100 bill at the office was considered nothing. It was hard, initially, to keep perspective because when I got home, $100 was a lot of money!

Q: It was substantial.
DONNA: Yes. And so it was very hard to differentiate between the two.

Q: So how did you deal with it?
DONNA: Just through experience. Getting that $100 bill at home and thinking "this isn't too bad" or "this is nothing" has definite consequences, like finding out that you're short at the end of the month for really important things!

There is one more thing I'd like to mention. The effect of all this money on the children.

Q: The children of traders?

Donna: Yes. It's a very big burden on them. Some of them have had a tremendously difficult time living up to the standards and successes of their parents. I've seen what that can do to people emotionally.

Q: And you are saying, Donna, that all these things have sobered your view about money?
Donna: Yes, very much. It made me want to change.

Q: Do you ever find yourself measuring your own self-worth as a human being by how much money you have?
Donna: Absolutely not!

Q: You know, of course, that a lot of people do.
Donna: Right. I know that my worth as a person is not measured by how much I have; it's what I do and how I live by God's law.

Q: What is most valuable to you in your life?
Donna: My faith and my family. I have found the peace and direction that I need in my life from having a relationship with Jesus. Any troubles that I've ever had—whether monetary or as a result of my first marriage—I now find the guidance and counsel that I need in the Word.

Q: Donna, what do you think is the ultimate purpose of money?
Donna: To help others. We have many ministries at our church that send money to people in third world countries like Bangladesh and India. Also to places where Christians are not able to enjoy religious freedom.

I believe I've seen both the positive and negative effects of money. I've seen what the money does constructively and how it helps people. I've also seen the evil money renders when it is not respected.

Q: Do you find that your personal values ever come into conflict with the world of high finance that you work in?

DONNA: Yes.

Q: Can you talk about that?

DONNA: In the past there were situations that occurred before I had my present philosophy, where I would say things like, "It's OK, that's just the way we do things here." But now I can't compromise my morals for monetary gain because in my heart that's not the right thing to do. Money is not the most important thing in the world! Morals and ideals and religious values come first.

Q: Donna, as it relates to your understanding of money, what do you think is the most important thing that you learned about yourself?

DONNA: That I shouldn't define my value by how much I have in my pocket, but rather by how much good I have in my heart. I think there's just such an overemphasis on money in American society. There's all the commercials and advertisements and just in general people are so obsesssed with impressing others with their material possessions.

This past weekend I attended a church seminar. The topic was hospitality. Do you know the difference between entertaining and hospitality? Entertaining is making sure that you have the right plates and settings, the floral arrangements and things like that. Hospitality is just inviting somebody over for a cup of coffee, not trying to impress them, just being welcoming. It allows others to find safety and security in your relationships.

Q: Donna, do you think when you were younger your attitude toward money was more in the entertaining mode, but now as your ideas have matured you are more oriented toward hospitality?

DONNA: Exactly! Today, the safety and security that I get from money does not derive from a need to impress. Now it's more like welcoming a neighbor, sharing a cup of coffee, trying to keep up a friendly relationship that is rooted in maturity and respect.

CHAPTER 11

Money Losses

Ira Sapir

Mr. Ira Sapir, 43, is a sculptor residing in New York City.

Q: Ira, what is your earliest memory of money?

Ira: This might land me in jail but here goes! I was four or five years old and my father, who was a hardworking immigrant who never went to school, used to keep a lot of change in his coat pocket. We lived in this old, long, narrow apartment and there was a delicatessen around the corner. They used to make these incredible chocolate-covered doughnuts. They were like bell-shaped cupcakes. I used to go into my father's pocket—I didn't even know what money was—and I'd get a whole handful of change and walk down to the street to buy those doughnuts. Of course, it was stealing, but I didn't know it to be that then. All I knew was I needed it to get my doughnuts!

Q: So your very earliest memory of money is reaching into your dad's coat pocket, mining for this magical substance that allows you to possess an object of your desire?

Ira: Yes. And I took handfuls, way more than I needed. I would keep it so I could go back another day and get more.

MONEY LOSSES

Q: What was your family's attitude toward money?

IRA: My father's attitude was simple: first you earned it, then you saved it, then you spent it. I didn't always do that, but that was really what I learned from him. My mother came from money, but it was wiped out during World War II. She was from Germany.

Q: And she lost all her money in the war?

IRA: Yes.

Q: As you were growing up, what were your thoughts about money? Did you feel it was important to have a lot of money?

IRA: No. A lot of money was never the issue. I worked from the time I was very young. I always worked so that I would have money in my pocket. So really, if I wanted something I would just earn it.

Q: Ira, do you remember any fantasies about money as you were growing up?

IRA: Not really, because even though my father didn't make a great deal of money he always took care of things. I mean, there was always enough food on the table. We had almost everything we wanted, and we weren't spoiled children.

Q: You never visualized yourself as a Donald Trump or somebody else who had a tremendous amount of money?

IRA: No. But I was also in the arts most of my life. I mean I've always worked and I've always had money in my pocket to buy things. Nothing luxurious, but if I wanted a bicycle or if I wanted a car I was always able to afford it. When I was 17 or 18, I started making glass, becoming a glassblower. I worked at a street fair and I made $600 in a weekend. I remember thinking that it was an incredible amount of money. My father wanted me to have a "profession," to be a lawyer. I remember him saying, "You're not going to be a glassblower to make a living." And I said, "Yes, I am. Just look how much money I made!"

Q: Your father didn't want you to become an artist?

IRA: He never went to school, so for him an education was extremely important. I have a brother who's a doctor and a brother who's a lawyer.

Q: So he wanted you to have a profession? Is that correct?

IRA: Yes. But I went into the arts. And I've always done OK.

Q: Ira, to what extent do you think that your feelings about money affected your career choice?

IRA: I think it has helped me as an artist to make a good living. I also had to prove to my family that I could make it. I'm not rich but I've always lived quite comfortably. It was always important to me to make a living. I never cared to be a starving artist!

Q: So you feel choosing this career path was, from the very beginning, motivated by practical considerations. In other words you didn't pursue some sort of romantic notion of art at all costs?

IRA: I did do it at all costs, but I also always kept up the practical end with it. For example, instead of taking the attitude about a work of sculpture that I'm going to put a price tag on it and say "Screw you if you don't pay up"! I've always been more practical. I'll say to myself, "Well, OK, I can get this price for it now and later on I'll be able to get more for another piece." I've always heard people say that's why I've done OK, because I have a pretty good business sense and I understand the value of money.

Q: Ira, from the beginning you haven't restricted yourself solely to the arts. You have tried your hand in a number of other things. Can you talk about that?

IRA: Bob, let's back up just a little bit. I was doing this glasswork in California and I was doing OK. This was 1980 or 1981 and I was making $80,000 to $100,000 a year. Today that doesn't seem like a lot of money, but for being in the art world at that point in time it was a pretty good living. Even so, I walked away from it. I had sold a piece to the Metropolitan Museum in New York City. It was one of those weird things where you gain a certain amount of success and you then feel you have to try something else. By a fluke I wound up in Chicago and started trading in the Standard & Poor's pit on the Mercantile Exchange.

IRA: I traded in the pit for about a year and a half. I remember losing five grand like boom! I dropped it in just a minute. It took me a long time to make it and I just lost it in the snap of a finger. I said to myself, "What's going on here?" Then the next thing I knew, I owned a nightclub.

Q: So you've always been kind of entrepreneurial. Is that right?

IRA: Right, I have always been involved in a lot of things in addition to my art. I mean, right now I have a trademark patent on a product in plastics.

Q: After you sold your nightclub you went back to doing your sculpture full-time?

IRA: In the beginning the nightclub was very successful and truthfully I had never seen money like that before. I mean I used to walk around with $5,000 in my pocket—chump change! And at that time I really didn't have anything to do with art at all except buying it from other people. I had the money to do it and I lived a really nice lifestyle.

Q: You used to walk around with $5,000? Did that give you a big rush?

IRA: Yes, an incredible rush. For the first time I was able to do whatever I wanted. I mean, it afforded me a lot of things. And I wasn't a very materialistic person. But I bought an Avanti. I don't know if you're familiar with that car. It's a strange car. I mean, I could have bought a Porsche like my partner or whatever. But an Avanti is where my taste was at. It was one of the few things I ever wanted and now was able to afford.

Q: Ira, would you say that owning the nightclub was a successful experience for you?

IRA: Yes, but it fell in the end and it wound up costing me a lot of money. Because in the end it went down. And instead of shutting the doors and getting out, I tried to save it and wound up losing most of my money.

Q: How did that experience affect your personal concept of money?

IRA: Well it affected me a lot because when I came to New York, I arrived with $10,000. That's all I had left. So I went from being successful in one field to being successful in another field making a great deal of money, only to having nothing to show monetarily for all my effort. When I returned to New York six years ago, basically I was starting from scratch.

Q: Ira, to what extent do you think you define yourself in terms of how much money you have?

IRA: I don't have a lot of money, but I can always take care of myself. Once you've had a lot of money, like I had with the nightclub, it's tough. I can't just go out now and drop a hundred bucks on dinner if I want. Those days are gone! Now I have to watch what I spend. I kind of miss that lifestyle.

Q: But to what extent do you think you tie your feelings of self-worth to your financial net worth?

IRA: A lot. It's a relevant issue.

Q: How do you deal with it?

IRA: Not very well, actually. You know, my sculptures sell for $25,000 to $30,000 apiece. Sounds like a lot of money but it's not after you consider how long each piece takes to make: two to three months. By the time everything is said and done, I haven't made very much. I would like to be able to spend a half a million or a million dollars on a building and lock myself in it. I would love to do that. I just can't, so it bothers me, you know.

Q: How much money do you think is enough?

MONEY LOSSES

IRA: If I was to make a $100,000 or $150,000 a year now I'd be very happy. I mean, I don't need millions. You know we all have our fantasies of what would happen if we won the lottery. If I won let's say $10 million in the lottery, I'd keep a mill for myself and set my brothers up and go into philanthropy. You know, set up a foundation.

Q: Ira, what do you think is the ultimate purpose of money?
IRA: Money is a means to an end.

Q: You had mentioned philanthropy and helping others. Do you see that as the purpose of money?
IRA: You know, Bob, making money is the easiest thing in the world. It's a mind-set. If I sat down and said, "Look, I'm going to make money" and that's all I wanted to do, it's not difficult to make money. The question is how much energy are you willing to commit and what are you willing to do to make it. For me, it's not a priority. Even though I would like to have it, it's really not a priority.

Q: What is most valuable to you?
IRA: Boy, I do not have an answer to that one. I've been trying to figure that out for myself.

Q: But you know it's not money per se?
IRA: Money is not the highest goal. Like I said, it's a means to an end. It's great to have it, it's nice to be able to do this and that. But money doesn't control me and it's not what I'm here for.

Q: To what extent do you think money has significantly affected the quality of your life?
IRA: Greatly. It's very relevant to it. When I have it, it does one thing; when I don't have it, it does another thing. Of course it affects me.

Q: Can you think of an important experience or event in your life where you felt you truly understood the true value of money?

IRA: About a year ago I split up with a woman I was with for seven years. Part of the separation was because of a building we were trying to buy. I had this money I had saved up for the past six or seven years since I got back on my feet. And it was just enough to put a downstroke on a building. We didn't get the building and it was sort of the beginning of the end. She wound up getting together with a pretty well-known musician. And I remember when I first heard about it, I thought "I can't compete with that." I used those very words because this guy makes good money, travels all over the world, and takes her with him. I often think, Damn, if I'd only been able to do things better, have a little more money, it would have made a difference! Not that this is necessarily true, but it was what I thought at the time.

Q: So you felt if you had more money you would have saved the relationship?

IRA: Yes. His feathers were brighter than mine. You know, it was like one of these animalistic things. And yeah, if I had made more money I would have been able to do this and do that and wouldn't have had to struggle so much.

Q: Ira, as it relates to your understanding of money, what do you think you learned most about yourself?

IRA: That I like it, and I need it. I understand its function and I wish I made more. Also that I used to think that it really didn't make a difference, but it does. I realize now that at my age I just can't continually start over again. I need to be able to secure things.

Q: What do you think it is about money that hangs us up so?

IRA: Money is a perception. It's security. You can see it in many aspects of life where individuals or situations are affected by it, when someone doesn't have enough money to pay his or her bills or to take care of what needs to be done. It puts a lot of stress into situations. Money provides peace of mind. And I think it's fascinating how it really affects people.

Q: Ira, do you find having money gives you peace of mind so that you can concentrate on your sculpture?

IRA: Sure it does. If I can pay my bills, which I do, and have enough left over to be comfortable, I'm not consumed with thinking about money. It also allows me to put all my energies into my work instead of thinking about having to pay my bills. So sure, it's very relevant.

CHAPTER 12

Reflections on a Pond

Bernadine Dohrn

MS. BERNADINE DOHRN, 49, is director of the Children and Family Justice Center. She is a former student radical who lived underground for 11 years.

Q: What is your earliest memory of money?

BERNADINE: Being taken by my father to open a savings account. It turns out to have been a futile gesture. I haven't had a savings account since.

Q: How old were you?

BERNADINE: Five, maybe. But I have a vivid memory of it. The bank was in the same building where my dentist was, so I had painful associations from the very start. Maybe that was the problem! My father, of course, was trying to teach me responsibility.

Q: How would you characterize your family's attitude toward money?

BERNADINE: I would characterize it as defining most of their life choices. Both my parents came from poor immigrant families and worked long and hard from the time they were teenagers. They were dedicated to giving my sister and me things that they never had an opportunity to experience. They were scrupulous about money and were never extravagant.

Q: Has that had an impact on you?

BERNADINE: Yes, of course, I became the exact opposite! I don't save money and I don't plan for the future. I spend all my money for the immediate term in order to have time together with my kids. Bob, I just remembered another childhood memory I would like to share. I remember standing in line with my mother for war rations. I have a clear memory of her winter coat and being at eye level with her legs. I think it's more of a memory of being young with my mother, but it's also tied to a feeling of an incredible sense of security that I think allowed me later to abandon the need for financial security.

Q: Bernadine, as you were growing up, do you remember having any particular thoughts or fantasies about money?

BERNADINE: I must have gotten an allowance at a certain point, because I have a strong memory of shopping for a present for my mother, whose birthday was always around Mother's Day. I remember being able to use my own coins to buy her a piece of jewelry. I must have been very young, and I must have gone with a neighbor to buy it for her. I can still picture picking out this little heart on a chain that I thought was fantastic. This memory is still very pleasant and "mothery." But at some point later I also remember becoming very angry, feeling that my father worked too long and hard and wasn't getting fairly compensated for all his effort.

Q: What did your father do?

BERNADINE: My father dealt with money. He was a credit manager for a variety of different businesses, but basically for appliance stores. In many ways he was the classic middleman, never making a lot of money himself, working long hours and extending and refusing credit to poor people.

Q: Bernadine, could you talk about your involvement in the student movement?

BERNADINE: Well, I actually didn't get involved until rather later. I was in law school and it was the civil rights movement and it was the sense of inequality I saw in the world that motivated me. Even though my parents certainly were lower middle class and not highly privileged, what drove me was not so much the anger I felt about my family's situation but rather what was going on in the country and the world. It drove me into some action that I didn't even understand the bigger implications of until much later.

Q: Do you think you were responding more to the inequalities that were based on social and racial grounds, or was it the monetary inequalities that you observed in terms of the differences between rich and poor in the country. Can you separate that in any way?

BERNADINE: It is hard to separate, isn't it?

Q: Yes, it is.

BERNADINE: My first perceptions of it was certainly on moral grounds. I remember still being in grade school watching the students on TV from Little Rock, Arkansas, marching through the National Guard and being spit upon and having paint thrown on them. I remember being shocked that this was being done also by white women. The idea that *they* could be attacking these little kids trying to go to school just completely horrified me.

Q: So, it was just the stark moral injustice of it, rather than any specific thoughts of economic inequality. . . .

BERNADINE: Yes. But I was exposed to that also. Before I went to law school I worked for a year as a caseworker for the Cook County Department of Public Aid. That for me was a real eye-opening year in terms of economic inequality!

Q: What was that like?

BERNADINE: It was in 1963, the year that President Kennedy was killed. I worked in the Englewood office, and my caseload, so to speak, was a public housing project on 26th and California, right across from the criminal courts building. It was a terribly poor population of single mothers. I would take two buses every day to get to the housing project and sit with these women in their kitchens, having instant coffee and going over their welfare checks which even then were impossible to live on!

Q: Do you remember thinking at the time about the monetary unfairness of the whole thing?

BERNADINE: Vividly, because my job was to go over the eligibility requirements with them. This was still in the days when the Welfare Department would conduct midnight raids to see if there were men's shoes in their closets! I would discuss with them whether they were eligible for winter coats for their kids or an extra bed or a crib. I would have to ask them questions about how much they were spending on food. I was shocked at how profoundly humiliating this process was for these women. I watched one woman go mad having her kids taken away from her.

Q: As you became more involved in the movement, how were you reacting to the economic disparities that you were witnessing?

BERNADINE: I came to feel it very personally. I believed my privilege was tied to their poverty. I felt we were all part of a connected system.

Q: Could you elaborate?

BERNADINE: I felt that this was an economic system that kept some people poor and some people rich, and it was wrong. . . . By the time Martin Luther King, Jr., came to Chicago, I was a law student and I was involved in organizing a city-wide rent strike. It became perfectly clear to me at the time that there were a few individuals who owned vast slum properties on the West Side. They failed to fix their buildings, and we organized against them. What we were doing was giving people a legal structure where they could put their rent money in escrow and then act as a tenants' union to fix up the buildings. People were hungry to do that and very active and very organized. It was astonishing how many buildings actually got organized and elected a tenants' union. We figured out ways to hire contractors in order to fix leaks and the electricity and make the buildings habitable.

Q: Bernadine, how do you think these experiences were shaping or affecting your personal understanding of the meaning of money?

BERNADINE: That year, I had the incredible luck to meet many organizers who had been working in the South. They were a vast array of very interesting and committed people. They had all been through many arrests and many difficult conditions that I couldn't even imagine! What stood out to me was that they were on a mission. They were not thinking about their careers or savings accounts or the pursuit of happiness. Everybody was living on what we used to call subsistence salaries, in apartments together, to pursue our goal.

Today, I'm constantly struck by the fact that even people who are doing what's called public interest work will almost never say, "Well, let's organize and do it" without asking first, "Well, where are we going to go for the money? Which foundation are we going to speak to?" In those days, nobody asked that. You didn't question who was going to underwrite our march into Cicero or Englewood. That was just not even an issue. We did it on a shoestring and on idealism and on a wish and a prayer, because we were right in principle, and that was more than enough!

Q: Bernadine, why do you think that is?
BERNADINE: Because we thought that the primary resource was human, not financial. People wouldn't ask how much they'd get

paid. They asked if there was work to be done. You see, what drove us was something much more important than money.

Q: What is your personal response to the climate of materialism in our contemporary culture?
BERNADINE: Well, I loathe it, and I'm also part of it. I don't know if it's the fact that I'm middle-aged or something, but I find it astonishing.

Q: Do you feel your participation has neutralized your earlier feelings of social concern?
BERNADINE: No, I don't, but I think that raising three children has neutralized it at least temporarily to an extent. Right now we're signing loans for our kids to go to college, and we're going to be working until we drop. With those bills that we have, the government will have an interest in us into our 90s. There will be no early retirement for us! We're going to be paying student loans forever.

Q: What about the materialism?
BERNADINE: As I look at contemporary American society I think there's two really corrosive things that have happened. One is the notion that what we do for pleasure, for recreation, for fulfillment, for being citizens, is *consumerism*. It's astonishing to me that people shop on their vacations. It's what they do. It's what they do when they go out on the weekend. It's even the way people express and define themselves! And the second thing that I feel has happened is that the culture has been tremendously successful at convincing the American people that we are economic animals— solely or primarily economic animals, rather than moral, intellectual, or social beings.

Q: Could you talk a little bit about your current work?
BERNADINE: About ten years ago I started doing children's law when we moved back to Chicago after being away for 20 years. I went to work representing abused and neglected children in Juvenile Court. This sort of put me right back into the old boat, where

the public welfare caseload was when I got out of college. It is the same population of the most impoverished kids and parents, with the same institutions—Cook County Hospital, the jails, and the courts. It's working with the poor and the dispossessed and seeing things from the kids' point of view.

Q: Could you talk a little bit about some of the monetary disparities that you continue to see?

BERNADINE: Well, I can give you one vivid example, because in the time that I've been doing this with other people's children and then coming home to my own kids, who are going to a private school, I see that the very same issues that are confronted by the kids in Juvenile Court—the same behaviors, the same circumstances—lead to utterly different life outcomes. So that daily contrast I guess helps fuel my outrage at the fact that the poor kids don't get the same chances and are seen by society as an utterly different form of being. And it's purely based on resources. You know, Bob, money is like a mark on your forehead. It's like a monetary sign of Cain that announces to the world whether you are one of the lucky or unlucky.

Q: Bernadine, based on your experiences in the movement, working with poor people and living underground outside the dominant economy for more than a decade, what do you think is the ultimate purpose of money?

BERNADINE: A couple of years ago when I spoke at a children's conference in Norway, I met James Grant, who was the head of UNICEF. He noted the fact that for the first time in human history there existed the wealth to feed the people of the world as well as to inoculate children against preventable diseases. There was enough surplus wealth and the mechanism to distribute it. So the only real question was one of moral will. I don't know if that's the ultimate purpose of money, but I believe it's what I feel money should be used for. To me it is an incredible irony that we feast upon news stories about violence and disaster and mayhem and ignore the silent violence, the lack of basic food, shelter, and health care.

Money is a kind of reflecting pond on which we, as human beings, can make significant choices. Things do not have to be the way they are! So why not basic equity first?

CHAPTER 13

Risky Business
John Monasta

MR. JOHN MONASTA, 45, is a professional blackjack player and financial futures trader. He resides in Santa Clara, California.

▼

Q: John, what is your earliest memory of money?

JOHN: I would say it goes back to doing little odd jobs around the house for an allowance. I think I learned from a very early age that for me money represented freedom, being able to do what you choose.

I was a real saver as a kid. I mean I would do my little work and just save and never spend any money at all. It was just ingrained in me that money was something important. If you had it, you could attain freedom. I knew from an early age that I didn't want to enter the corporate rat race and that the freedom money could buy was essential to me. So, from an early age, that's really what money has meant for me.

Q: What was your family's attitude toward money?

JOHN: My dad was a professor at Santa Clara University. He was kind of middle class, I guess you would say. Money was important, but it wasn't like where we were always trying to keep up with the Joneses or anything remotely like that.

Q: Money wasn't a driving force; you didn't feel you suffered from a scarcity of money, nor was it something that was a major motivating factor in your early childhood. Is that correct?

JOHN: That's exactly correct. You hit the nail right on the head. I've never really had any tremendous desire to drive the biggest car or live in the biggest house. But on the other hand, I certainly want to stay away from the wrong side of town, too!

Q: As you were growing up, did you feel it was important to have a lot of money?

JOHN: Not really. As I said before, I was always more of a saver. I wasn't the type of guy who went out and blew his money on girls or spent it on a car or bought tons of records.

Q: John, I will say you have really changed my initial impression of what I would have thought the early experiences and attitudes of a professional gambler would have been. I certainly would not have thought that the training ground that produced a saver would also produce a professional gambler. But that obviously seems to be your experience.

JOHN: Yeah, you wouldn't think that. Actually I got involved in professional gambling just by accidentally coming across a book of my dad's called *The Casino Gambler's Guide*. He simply had it because he was also in the insurance business. There was some discussion of mathematics in there that interested him.

Q: As you were growing up did you have any fantasies about money?

JOHN: Oh, yeah. I fantasized about having great houses all around the world. Being able to just get on my yacht and sail away whenever I wanted to. But I really never had this tremendous desire to turn those fantasies into reality. I think fantasy is a good word!

Q: So you were content to have them reside on the level of fantasy knowing that it was fantasy?

JOHN: Exactly. Of course, Bob, I still wouldn't mind having those things, but it hasn't been an overwhelming desire for me to accumulate tremendous amounts of wealth. I mean, you can only live in one house at a time and drive one car at a time. Quite frankly, the security and freedom to basically do whatever I want is much more important than just accumulating a lot of material things.

Q: How would you characterize your current relationship with money?

JOHN: We probably haven't known each other well enough.

Q: You and money?

JOHN: Exactly. I mean, I've certainly had money but . . .

Q: So it's an estranged relationship? Or it's a strange relationship?

JOHN: I'd say estranged at the present time. That's one thing about gambling and speculation. You certainly have your ups and your downs, which again I think is why you have to kind of take a fairly realistic view about it. You don't want to get overexcited when you're doing well nor sink into the depths of depression when you're not.

Q: John, what do you think drew you to the life of a professional gambler?

JOHN: Probably two main things, Bob. One was that, living in the San Francisco Bay area, we were just four hours from Lake Tahoe. As a kid, we went up there a lot on vacations. Just being around the few casinos they had up there, I found the atmosphere tremendously exciting. Even though I couldn't go in and play, just walking through the casinos and seeing the excitement was a huge high.

Q: What did you find so exciting?

JOHN: Gosh, just the lights and the excitement of all the people milling around, standing at the craps table yelling and screaming, watching all that money constantly changing hands. It was really exciting for me! Probably more like the excitement that other people get from watching the Kentucky Derby. And then as I mentioned when I came upon this book of my dad's, *The Casino Gambler's Guide*, I saw that one could make money by counting cards at blackjack. I thought to myself, "Ah-hah, this is for me." And I'd say those are the two main things that got me started down this path.

Q: What happened next?

JOHN: I guess I was probably about 18 the first time I ever went into one of the clubs and played. Of course, this was after not only reading *The Casino Gambler's Guide* but also studying it and rigorously practicing its techniques at home. I probably spent twice as much effort studying gambling than I did studying my academic courses at college.

Q: So you were really a student of gambling. I mean, this was not something you took lightly, this was a serious enterprise for you.

JOHN: Absolutely. That's the only way that I think one can head down that road and have any chance of success at all. I mean, hundreds of thousands of people have read books on how to count cards in blackjack. But probably $1/10$ of 1 percent have had any kind of reasonable success, not to mention doing it for a living. It was a very, very serious undertaking and I practiced it for several hours each day for many years before I went up to the casinos. In the beginning I got tossed out maybe once a month because I wasn't even 21 yet. But I managed to get enough experience and started playing for $1 to $5 a hand, just the absolute minimum bets to get the practice and experience I needed.

Q: How did you do?

JOHN: At first not very well. There's a lot to it. A lot of concentration and quite frankly, in blackjack one has to play many, many hours because your edge is so small. And at first, like I said, I did not do too well. But I'm a very determined guy when I get it into myself that I want to do something. It actually took me two to three years before I was able to win consistently.

Q: When you say you began to win consistently, what do you mean by that?

JOHN: I would say that most of my success came in playing with groups of others, rather than going into a casino and playing on my own. And winning consistently meant going to Nevada and playing for maybe a week or so and virtually never losing.

Q: You mean you play with a team of other professional blackjack players?

JOHN: That's correct.

Q: What do you think are the keys to successful game playing?

JOHN: I'd say the most important one is not to make any mistakes. Be 100 percent accurate in your playing because your edge is so small.

Q: Accurate to your system and strategy you mean?

JOHN: Exactly. Not making mistakes counting the cards, not making mistakes in your betting strategy, not making mistakes in playing the hand correctly. That is the "secret" for doing well. Also, money management, which kind of goes along with not making mistakes. You know, not betting or overbetting when you're losing.

Q: In your judgment, John, how do you think the experience of being a professional gambler shaped your personal concept of money?

JOHN: Quite frankly in a negative manner because I probably don't have the respect for money that I should have. You go into a casino with a few thousand dollars and you train yourself not to think of thousands of dollars as money: they're just units. In other words, when I first started to play I wasn't playing dollars. They were just dollar units. Later on if we were playing for $500 a hand, each unit was $500. It wasn't money!

Q: And you made money consistently?

JOHN: That's correct. And so you know, probably one of my biggest faults is I don't have the respect for money that I should and maybe don't have some of the deep desires that I should as far as accumulating wealth. Quite frankly, 90 percent of what I think about money is just a bankroll to either play blackjack or trade commodities with.

Q: Is it the risk that you enjoy so much?

JOHN: Actually not. I'm not really a big risk taker. In fact, with the exception of what I do for a living, for me a big bet would be to bet $25 on the Super Bowl. Honest to God, I'm not a big gambler.

Q: But you'll play cards for $500 a hand?

JOHN: Exactly. And sometimes a lot more than that. So we're talking fairly big stakes. And yet again in real life, for me a big bet is $5 on a football game. Or if I go out and play golf, I'll bet my brother no more than $1 a hole or something like that.

Q: But when you bet your brother $1 a hole, there can't be a lot in it for you psychologically. Is that correct?

JOHN: That's probably true, but what happens is I do concentrate a little harder. The game becomes a lot more fun because there is something riding on it. It's not anything significant, but I'm a tremendously competitive person. I just can't stand to lose! So just by betting something, even if it's something very small, brings out the competitive nature in me. I find it much more enjoyable to play under those circumstances for a little money than to just go out and play.

Q: What do you think is the ultimate purpose of money?

JOHN: Well, naturally, it's a representative of either wealth or potential wealth or just anything that you might want to get. In other words, $10 represents three packs of cigarettes, or whatever. For somebody else, looking at it on a bigger scale, $3 million would represent, "Well gee, I can go out and buy a great yacht or a pretty nice home." Or to another person, $3 million might be, "Hey, I can put it in some little account and draw the interest off it and be able to retire in a relatively comfortable manner."

Q: So what is its ultimate purpose for John Monasta?

JOHN: I would say my main goal regarding accumulating money would be to have enough so I could have a reasonable interest income and wouldn't have to worry about making more money. And yet at the same time, I would be able to trade commodities and view it more as just a game rather than as a means to make money to pay this month's mortgage payment.

Q: Can you think of an important experience or event in your life where you thought you gained a better understanding about the meaning of money?

JOHN: I'd say one time in Carson City. I was just kind of getting to one of those next plateaus. I was moving from playing dollars to playing thousands of dollars. You don't just do it in one step. And we had a pretty big win there. We won about $30,000 and it just kind of propelled me to the next level. And I kind of knew at that point that there was no looking back. I had, let's say, arrived. And that to me was a really important thing. I think that you know, one needs a certain amount of success to be successful. And that for me was an important watermark in my progress.

Q: As it relates to your understanding of money, John, what do you think is the most important thing you learned about yourself?

JOHN: I would say one thing for sure is the way I look at money. Growing up as a kid, you always think, Gosh, I want to be a millionaire. I want to have a million dollars. So for a long time I always just thought, I want to try to accumulate a lot of money. But as I became older, I just realized that what I needed was a relatively steady source of income; that would be a lot more important than just accumulating a specific amount. I'd say that that's one of the most important things that I've changed about myself regarding money.

Q: That you just need a steady income of money?

JOHN: Exactly. Rather than just saying, "Well yeah, as soon as I get a million dollars, I'm going to be happy or I'm going to have accomplished my goal." Again I think that for me money is more a means to an end and that end, just like it was in the beginning, is to obtain freedom.

Q: The same freedom you wanted when you were a little kid.

JOHN: Exactly. It's really exactly the same. And I've never wanted to get to the point where having a lot of money was going to cause problems. I mean, I kind of laugh to myself sometimes when you see some celebrity is getting paid $15 million for a picture. And another guy says, "Well you know, if he's going to get $15 million, then I'm going to get 20. I'm not going to make another picture until I get 20!" I mean, that type of stuff to me is just silly beyond belief. I mean, you've already got more money than you could ever possibly spend anyway and you end up causing yourself emotional grief because you start to get upset about it. I've never wanted to be in that kind of situation.

Q: Why do you think people allow themselves to get into that mind frame?

JOHN: Maybe it's a competitive nature, just like me being competitive in a small way on the golf course. I guess for the superwealthy, their competitive nature comes out with being better than the next guy in their profession. You know, whether it's an attorney or a fellow who produces pictures. And the money is just the box score.

Q: Kind of reminds me of that T-shirt we used to see in the 1980s: HE WHO HAS THE MOST TOYS AT THE END WINS.

JOHN: It's kind of funny that you mentioned that because I had actually thought of that myself during our conversation. Except I saw that on a license plate frame rather than on a T-shirt. But that really is what it reminds me of, too.

Q: John, what would you say is a good metaphor for your personal concept of money?

JOHN: Boy, that's a good question. I would go back to the idea of freedom and security. To me money represents a nice, warm, cozy home that I can live in. A place where I would feel warm and safe.

Q: Security.

JOHN: Exactly.

Q: It's very interesting that someone who spends his life as a professional gambler would choose safety and security as his metaphor for money. But I guess in another way it makes a lot of sense.

JOHN: Well it is kind of interesting. But remember when I go out and play I virtually never lose. I mean, to me gambling is one of the most secure ways to make a living. There's certainly a lot less stress or risk in gambling than worrying if you're going to get laid off!

CHAPTER 14

You Be the Judge
Michele Lowrance

JUDGE MICHELE LOWRANCE is a circuit court judge for the city of Chicago who presides over family court matters.

Q: Michele, what is your earliest memory of money?
MICHELE: My earliest memory about money is associated with a particular kind of shoe, Papagalos, that I had to have when I was a student in the 1960s at Miami Beach High School. They cost $11.95. If you didn't have them, you weren't accepted. I knew that having money related to owning those shoes.

Q: Was it the cool kids who wore them or the rich ones?
MICHELE: The cool kids, because at that point I didn't make a distinction about who was rich and who wasn't. I just knew who had the shoes and who didn't.

Q: What was your family's attitude toward money?
MICHELE: My grandfather was the head interior designer for John Wanamaker's in Philadelphia. He was very showy in his personal attire, and he dressed my grandmother lavishly. She was very stylish and would wear jade with her green dresses and sapphires with her blue ones. I never heard him evaluate anybody on the

MONEY TALKS

basis of money, however. I never heard that kind of talk in my house.

Q: As you were growing up, did you feel it was important to have a lot of money?

MICHELE: No, not at all. I thought it was important to have enough money for food because there was a scarcity of food in my house when I was growing up.

Q: You say there was a scarcity of money?

MICHELE: There was money, it just wasn't being spent. After my grandfather died when I was 12, my grandmother just stopped spending money. She stopped buying clothes, food, everything. I remember her asking, "Where is the money now going to come from?" It was all about scarcity.

Q: Did you have any childhood fantasies about money?

MICHELE: I don't recall any.

Q: Do you believe money is the root of all evil or the sum of all blessings?

MICHELE: I don't really deal in blanket statements like that because they deny all the shades of gray. I think money is about the trickiest issue there is and more than likely it's corrupting.

Q: As a family court judge, you preside over cases that involve financial settlements where people come to grips over money, is that true?

MICHELE: Yes.

Q: How would you characterize the role of money in the lives of the people who come before your court?

MICHELE: Money is integrally tied to fear. And the way I see it is that people believe that money will buy them a cushioned existence so that all of the hard and rough spots of life will be buffered. In fact, that may be true, which is what's good about money—but it is also what's bad about it. Too much buffering means you don't involve your soul.

Q: Well, I know personally, Michele, you've seen lots of money. You were married to a very well-known commodities broker and you know firsthand what the social world of high finance is all about.

MICHELE: I truly do.

Q: Based on your personal background and professional experience, how would you characterize your understanding of money?

MICHELE: I think it's very rare to see individuals who are extremely successful monetarily who know how to enjoy their lives. The dues that they have paid to get to where they are financially generally leave a gap in their character. To evolve in life you have to attend to that. What I hear people say all the time in and out of my courtroom is that they're going to put in their dues now and later they'll have a good time and enjoy themselves. The problem with that is when later comes, they are creatures of their own habits. They're transformed into prisoners of their own perceptions. Later is too late!

Q: How would you characterize your current relationship with money?

MICHELE: Well, it's a good question, because when I was practicing law I was making substantially more than I'm making now. I had the entrepreneurial spirit. When you're a lawyer you always believe that the "big case" is just around the corner. But as a judge, you're salaried. It's not a bad salary, but I soon found I had to do a budget. I never did that before, but it's infinitely better for me. The things I've loved best in my life are never the things that have made me money.

Q: We'll talk about that in a minute, but first I want to ask you to what extent do you feel others define you in terms of how much money you have?

MICHELE: To be a judge is sort of an aberration because you get defined in a certain way: you get a lot of respect. But you don't receive a huge amount of money. That is quite different from what most people in the world ever experience.

Q: To what extent do you define yourself in terms of how much money you have?

MICHELE: I don't. I define myself in terms of my positive impact on others.

Q: When you were a lawyer you didn't feel others defined you in terms of your material success?

MICHELE: I'm sure they did, but I'm a woman, so it's easier for me to make less and have less. It's not the same as it is for a man. But frankly I didn't feel the pressure because I didn't pay attention to it. It was not an issue for me.

Q: It has never been an issue for you?

MICHELE: Never been my hot button. Now to be candid, I do want to show up in a wonderful-looking suit. I do want to look good. I would experience shame if I thought I didn't look well dressed. So I do need a certain amount of money to get that off the ground.

Q: But you get that with the respect and deference from being a judge, right?

MICHELE: No, I need the good outfit, too!

Q: Deference isn't enough?

MICHELE: It's not enough, no. And I need to travel.

Q: What is most valuable to you and why?

MICHELE: That's easy. The positive blueprint that I leave on people's lives and the intimate relationships that I have with my friends and family. Those are the most valuable things, far and above everything else. I suppose if I weren't healthy, it would also be my health.

Q: Do you ever think about how much money you have? Is that something that you think about?
MICHELE: Yes.

Q: In what way?
MICHELE: I think about it in terms of making sure that I figure out a way so that I have money for when I'm older, because I know there are things I'm going to want to do. I also think about not being irresponsible. I try to view my life in a cohesive way financially. I try to conserve.

Q: Did you get that from your grandmother?
MICHELE: After my divorce, I went to law school in 1970. There were only two women in my year out of a class of several hundred. I figured out a way to take care of myself. You know, God bless the child that's got his own and all of that! That came out of being brought up in an environment of scarcity.

Q: How much money do you think is enough?
MICHELE: Enough would be to live off the interest and be able to be comfortable.

Q: But you don't think in terms of a number. You just think about it in terms of the lifestyle that you want. Is that right?
MICHELE: Right. And I don't want villas or anything remotely like that.

Q: So it's not about accumulation?
MICHELE: It would be boring! Can you imagine owning a villa here and a villa there. It would be just too much effort.

Q: Michele, I know that you know people who have accumulated pretty sizable fortunes. How do you relate to that?

MICHELE: I think that too can be OK. Everybody should get to do what they want to do in life. As long as you're taking care of the people in your life—thinking about some spiritual connection, some purpose, living a life with meaning other than accumulation—then you can acquire all you want to. I do my best not to judge, but it's hard. Occasionally, I want to shake some of my friends and say, "Don't you want to just have a good time? Why don't you travel? Why don't you go do something meaningful and stop just living to make money?"

Q: What is money's ultimate purpose for you?

MICHELE: To use it in a way that offers you the opportunity to live a life of meaning. Does that make sense?

Q: What does that mean to you: "to live a life of meaning?"

MICHELE: Well to me, waking up in the morning, trying to figure out what I was going to buy or acquire would make me feel very empty. One of my goals now is to produce a medical show raising people's awareness about health issues. That would be money really well spent. Caring for needy children. You know, having a big facility where you can take in foster children. That's money well spent! I don't mean to sound like I'm Mother Theresa. I am far from it! Look, I just bought a new bracelet—I'm there, too!

Q: But for you the ultimate purpose of money would be to do good and leave your imprint, as you put it. Is that correct?

MICHELE: Yes, and look good while I'm doing it!

Q: Wear a nice suit?
MICHELE: Exactly.

Q: To what extent do you think money has significantly affected the quality of your life?

YOU BE THE JUDGE

MICHELE: When I was a lawyer, my life revolved around making money. But the quality of my life was nowhere near what it is now.

Q: So the quality of your life is not proportional to the amount of money you make?

MICHELE: I'd go further. For me, it seems that making less and not having my life revolve around money has increased the quality of my life dramatically.

Q: How do you account for that?

MICHELE: It's great being a judge. That's how I account for my increased quality of life. Being a judge is just so immensely stimulating. The compensation is far beyond any monetary rewards.

Q: Can you think of an important event or experience in your life where you felt you truly came to know the true value of money?

MICHELE: Recently I lost my best friend of 37 years to cancer. Money necessary to secure a special nurse was what it would take so that she wouldn't suffer. I went right to the deep edge of understanding what money is all about. I was able to fly down to Florida to see her because I had the money to do it. To help buy her certain comforts made all the difference. In that moment when her pain was no longer tolerable, to have the money to buy her way out of that physical pain . . . money really did matter!

Q: Do you feel this was a defining moment for you in terms of how you view money?

MICHELE: Yes, because it was just so real. The reality is that you've got to put some money away for these kinds of eventualities because we're all mortal and anybody can be diagnosed with cancer, and that's real. And I've tasted it and I've smelled it. It made an impact on me that is profound. It also made me think critically about issues relating to money, like the questions you are asking me. I learned that I'm not immune from having to think about these things in a responsible way.

Q: Why do you think people get so hung up about money?

MICHELE: For most people money is a scorecard. It's like "Here's my scorecard and I have to wear it right on the front of my T-shirt." So how I portray myself and the illusion of what my bank account is, is how I'm going to feel about myself. This is America after all and we wear it out in public all of the time!

Have you considered if you want to change your perspective from being material to more spiritual, let's say, from what source in our society would you learn it from? If you wanted to change your values, where would you go? I mean, would you go see your rabbi or your priest? Which friends of yours would you talk to? Where is the support for that kind of thing? If you were to go around talking about value and nonmaterialism, as an American you would be viewed as a flake. So what is the incentive to swim upstream, given that you're going to be viewed negatively? Who is going to give you the map and where would you take that journey?

We are the product of so much materialism and mass marketing. We are marketed to every single solitary day of our lives. And no one is challenging us to look at our inner selves and see how we're doing and what have we done for someone else lately. What if we were routinely exposed to that message? Just think, then, how different American culture would be.

CHAPTER 15

The Ultimate Buzz

Jim Nicodem

MR. JIM NICODEM is the senior pastor of Christ Community Church, a nondenominational congregation of 1,800 in St. Charles, Illinois. He is 42 years old, married, and the father of three children.

Q: Jim, what is your earliest memory of money?

JIM: That's a good question, Bob. I can't say that I honestly recall. Probably working for an allowance as a child, doing chores around the house, and getting paid for it.

Q: Where'd you grow up?

JIM: Mount Prospect, Illinois.

Q: What was your family's attitude toward money?

JIM: I would say very structured and very frugal. My father made a good income. He was the president of a small insurance company. But in spite of that, the money was spent very carefully.

Q: As you were growing up, do you remember having any specific thoughts about money?

JIM: No, I don't honestly recall feeling one way or another. On the one hand, there was not poverty about us, so I wasn't thinking,

Boy, if we just had more money, we could be more comfortable. On the other hand, the way we spent money was not extravagant. Consequently I wasn't thinking in terms of huge dreams that could be accomplished with it. Money really wasn't a huge part of my consciousness! My needs were met. Most of my clothes were hand-me-downs from my older brother. So again, despite the fact that I'm sure we could have afforded certain things, we didn't buy them. For example, we never ever spent a dime traveling on vacation. If we went someplace, we never flew. For years we went camping. And in later years when we traveled to Florida, we would rent an economy hotel room where we could do our own cooking and everything else. So even when we did spend money, it was always very carefully.

Q: Do you believe money is the root of all evil, or is that too simplistic?

JIM: I would say, first of all, that we've got to get our quote correct, because the scriptural quote is "The love of money is the root of all evil." I would not say that money itself is the root of evil, but I would say that a person's disposition toward it could be either very complementary to his or her life or very injurious.

Q: Jim, I'll give you an opportunity in a moment to talk more about that, but first I'd like to ask you another question. How would you characterize your current relationship with money?

JIM: On the one hand, I would say much like my childhood, because I have a comfortable income, and the church remunerates me quite fairly. I don't really worry about it a whole lot. As far as my kids' college fund is concerned, we're setting aside money for that. I'm not worried about whether or not we're going to afford meals or clothes or whatever; we seem to do all right on that. On the other hand, I'm still characterized by that same kind of frugality. We don't make excursions to the shopping mall. We don't like spending a whole lot of money for a vacation. We try to do things that we can do for free for entertainment. So on a personal level, we're living comfortably. Money is a commodity used in trade to get what we need, but there's certainly no extravagance, nor is there any poverty for us that is attached to it. Bob, I really encounter money more in my job as a pastor. For me, it's probably the number one indicator of where a person's heart is, spiritually.

Q: Jim, how do you relate to the issue of money in terms of the spiritual needs of your congregation?

JIM: As a congregation, we have grown immensely in a dozen years. When we started we had six couples; we have now grown to 1,800 people at a weekend service. In that time, we've bought 40 acres of land with three building projects. So on the one hand, money has been a very significant vehicle for meeting the needs of our expansion. On the other hand, I can honestly say that money is not my biggest concern where people are concerned. I don't see myself as a fund-raiser! I don't feel pressure in that regard. I really do believe that if we're doing what God wants us to do, He's going to see to it that our needs are met. On the other hand, money is a very big deal, because I see it not as a means of getting what we need churchwise, I see it as an indicator of where a person's heart is. And we live in such an affluent culture, and money is such a big deal to people, that to me, whether or not they're givers or takers says a lot about what God's doing in their hearts right now.

Q: Could you elaborate on that a little bit more, Jim?

JIM: Sure. You know, a scripture that comes to my mind, Bob, is the most familiar New Testament scripture, the one that even the guys at the sporting events hold up on the big placard, John 3:16, which begins by saying that "God so loved the world that He gave his only son." And what that tells me is that God's basic character is a giving character. So if I want to see whether the character of God is reflected in people's lives, I need to look at their generosity. Are they givers like God? Or are they hoarders? So to me, in part, I judge my success as a pastor by whether or not my people are becoming givers. You know, there's a baseline that scripture talks about, namely the tithe, that 10 percent of one's income is earmarked as the Lord's, and that's merely a reflection of the fact that in truth He owns it all. I don't want people tied down to the legality of a 10 percent figure. I would love to think that that's almost a starting place, and that beyond that, people see the needs of the world around them, giving to ministry opportunities, providing for world relief opportunities and so on.

Q: Jim, do you ever find yourself judging people in terms of how much they give to the church or its causes?

JIM: I think "judging" would be too harsh a word, because I think it's a pejorative word. I use money as a yardstick. Am I helping these folks to imbibe biblical principles? Is the character of Christ being formed in them? If not, then I've got a job to do still, and I need to make sure that they understand that if they're truly going to follow Christ wholeheartedly, they've got to be givers. Jesus didn't come to take, He came to lay his life down as a ransom for people. So if we're going to reflect His character in our lives, it must be characterized by generosity. But I do see it also as a judgment on me. And I would also say, I see it as a gauge of where people are in their spiritual journey.

Q: Jim, what would you say is the ultimate purpose of money?

JIM: I'd say absolutely to serve and help others. That's what the Apostle Paul said in II Corinthians 8 and 9, the chapters on money. He talks about the fact that by God's grace you'll abound in order to help others. And I would say, God prospers me in order that I can be generous with others as well.

Q: How do you respond to contemporary American culture with its emphasis on consumerism?

JIM: I respond to it almost as viscerally as I do to the immorality I see around me. I'm very disturbed at immorality in the media, in the sitcoms, in the movies, in the magazines, etc. I would put money and the abuse of money, and the extravagant way we spend it on ourselves, in the same category. It makes my stomach churn, and you know, I see it as the biggest obstacle to people coming to face God and following Him wholeheartedly. There is the story in the Gospel of the young rich man who comes to Jesus and wants to follow Him. And Jesus, kind of as a test to see how serious he is, tells him what to do. He says, "Go sell all you have, give it to the poor, and then come follow me." Now there's no other account in scripture where Jesus says something similar to anybody. We can guess it wasn't Jesus' standard fare—if you want to be a follower of mine, you've got to sell everything! However in this young man's case, it seems there's every indication it was a critical test. You know, what does this guy love most in life? And Jesus hit the nail on the head, it was his money! And he refused to do it. The scripture says he turned and he walked away, and Jesus looked at him with love. I think Christ really loved this guy but recognized that there was no way this man was going to make a priority out of following God until he dealt with the money monster in his life.

Q: Do you think we'd all be better if we gave away our money?

JIM: No, I think we would be better if we were givers, but I don't by any means feel it's necessary to give it all away. Some of the most generous people in the world I know are very wealthy people. It's just that they're not dominated by their money. Some of the stingiest people I know are people who don't have a whole lot. So to me it's a heart thing. You can have a lot and still be an incredibly generous giver. You could have very little and withhold.

Q: As it relates to your understanding of money, Jim, what do you think it is that you most learned about yourself?

JIM: That's a good question, Bob. You know, maybe it's the deceitfulness of money. I mean, we could talk all we want about the right thing to do with money with regard to generosity, but even as I'm talking to you I'm recognizing that I'm indicting myself. I still wrestle with my own standard of living. I live in an upper-middle-class community. Living in this community requires that I live in a house in an affluent community, drive a car, etc. There are many times that I wrestle with the affluence. And compared with the community, we live frugally. It still bothers me that money has as much a grip on me as it does.

Q: We live in a material culture where people are not only defined by how much they have, but internally, we develop feelings of self-worth based on our net worth. So, it's very understandable why we have to wrestle with this issue. It is also, I believe, the challenge. Jim, what do you think it is about money that hangs people up so?

JIM: I truly think it's what we think money buys, and also, like the old philosopher said, we've all been born with a God-size vacuum in our lives that never gets filled until God fills it. We have a propensity to try and fill that vacuum with money and stuff.

Q: So, it's our own insecurity that hangs us up?

JIM: Maybe significance more than security.

Q: No, I said insecurity.

JIM: Right, but what I'm saying is, I'm not sure that we're trying to buy security as much as we're trying to buy something that gives us a buzz. So, you know, if I'm feeling bad, I go out to the mall and I buy something new. Or you go to the car lot, and you look for something that'll make you feel good to drive. I think we're all looking for that buzz. I think the ultimate buzz comes from knowing Christ and being in a relationship with God. The hang-up is trying to fill that hole with stuff that doesn't satisfy us long term, because it rusts or it gets stolen or it breaks or it goes out of style or whatever. It's just a temporary fix.

Q: And Christ never rusts.

JIM: Yeah! Exactly.

CHAPTER 16

As Simple as ABC

Kenny Dichter

MR. KENNY DICHTER, 30, is president and CEO of Alphabet City Records. He resides in New York City.

Q: Kenny, what is your earliest memory of money?

KENNY: I guess my earliest memory of money is my dad handling it. When I think of money, I think of my dad. I remember him teaching me how to add and subtract. I also remember making change for the grown-ups and everybody thinking it was cute.

Q: As you were growing up, do you remember having any particular thoughts about money?

KENNY: I grew up in an upper-middle-class neighborhood on Long Island where money was evident. You knew who had it and you knew who didn't have it. I remember that I wanted it. I didn't know why, but I knew that I did!

Q: So as you were growing up, you thought it was important to have a lot of money?

KENNY: I wouldn't say a lot, but like I said, you knew the difference between who had it and who didn't. Having money meant a bigger house, a bigger car, you know, out to dinner every night—

that type of thing. I guess at a young age I was looking to be one of those guys.

Q: Are you saying you wanted to be the guy who had a lot of money?
Kenny: Yeah.

Q: Did you have any particular fantasies about money?
Kenny: Well, I think other people have the dream of kicking off their shoes in their huge office and telling everybody what to do. You know, being the man, the big daddy, the guy who calls the shots.

Q: So you're living your dream now?
Kenny: I would say I'm about 25 percent there. When I was a kid watching *Gilligan's Island,* I related to two people: Thurston Howell III and the professor.

Q: So which one did you choose in terms of a career path?
Kenny: I guess early on, the professor, and I'm looking to retire as Thurston Howell III.

Q: How would you characterize your current experience with money?
Kenny: I live and work in New York City where money plays a very important role in what you get to do. I mean, if you don't have it, you're sitting at home watching HBO; if you have it, you're out at some of the greatest restaurants and exposed to some of the greatest culture in the world. I mean, yes, you can go to a museum or have cheap thrills. But in New York, "money makes the world go around." It's just a way of keeping score.

Q: So you prefer to have the expensive thrills as opposed to the cheap ones.
Kenny: You know what's funny is I have a fantasy of the expensive thrills, but I think my thrills are the same as they were when I

was 15: playing ball, making love, eating food—you know, that kind of stuff. But it's just nice to know that you can do it if you want to.

Q: Kenny, to what extent do you feel other people define you in terms of how much money you have, and to what extent do you feel you define yourself?

KENNY: I think on the outside, if somebody just looked at me, their first thought is probably not, "This guy's loaded." But I do think people sense that I have success in what I do. I also know that I can play the perception game as well as anybody else. I think if I have $1 million, they probably think I have $10 million.

Q: Do you think other people judge you by how much money you have?

KENNY: I would say everybody judges people to an extent. That's not my biggest indicator when I look at somebody, but I've got to believe that a portion of the population does view me that way.

Q: To what extent do you think you judge yourself, I mean, just internally?

KENNY: It's just a way of keeping score. I mean, I really feel I've been blessed to be able to live and to do the things that I like to do. But I think when you talk about, the keeping score aspect, it's nice to know you've got X amount or Y amount in the bank.

Q: How much money do you think is enough?

KENNY: I mean, at 30? I'll say if you had 50 or 100, you probably don't have to worry about anything—and I mean million. If you speak to people that have 100 or 200, they'll say 500, so who knows?

Q: What is most valuable for you right now?

KENNY: My wife, my health, my family. Money is secondary when you ask me what's important when it comes up against stuff like that.

Q: Kenny, in your universe of values, what do you think is the ultimate purpose of money?

KENNY: I think money equals freedom. I think you go through a whole lot trying to making money so you don't have to worry about money. That's a very, very condensed way of saying it.

Q: Kenny, right now you're at an interesting juncture in your career. You started up a business, Alphabet City Records, from scratch, and it is just at the point where it is about to go public. Can you elaborate?

KENNY: Right now I'm at a very interesting place in my career. I'd say I'm at a "Y" in the road. You know, basically we're an entrepreneurial company doing a few million dollars in sales and have an opportunity to sell to a much larger entity—take a little bit of risk off the table and put some money in our pockets. Literally to become millionaires overnight.

Q: What does that feel like?

KENNY: It's exciting. You know, I guess that's sort of a barrier for everybody. You know, even though in 1950 it probably would have been a lot more than it is now in 1998. I think when you get there you no longer have to worry about your water bill or your cable TV bill every month. I think it takes you to a different echelon of freedom, and I think it'll allow me to be more creative by freeing me up from not worrying about the little things that most people have to contend with.

Q: To what extent do you think money has significantly affected the quality of your life thus far?

KENNY: I don't think it has. I think I'm doing everything I want to do. I don't think money is the answer to everything. I think you've got to have inner peace. I think money makes things a little bit easier. I love the David Geffen quote: "Anybody who thinks money solves all their problems doesn't have money." You know, 98 percent of the people you speak to who don't have money would argue with that, and I'm sort of in the middle right now. You know, I'm actually right at the crux. I want to know, when I have that money, how am I going to feel? Will I feel any different? I really don't know. So, maybe there's a little anxiety to that.

Q: So you're right at the point of finding out?
KENNY: Well, Bob, you got me right at the crux, because . . .

Q: Right on the threshold.
KENNY: Yes. They're announcing the deal on Wednesday. You'll probably read it in the *Wall Street Journal.*

Q: Kenny, how do you think being in the business that you're in has shaped your personal concept of money?
KENNY: The business that I'm in is sports and music. There's silly money in sports and there's silly money in music, meaning that 18- or 20-year-old kids are running around with $20 million; or being advanced a terrific amount of money by executives in order for them to perform their services. It's all a little bit unreal. I went to school in Madison, Wisconsin, where, if you made 75 or a 100 grand a year, you were considered a wealthy person. I think being in this industry has skewed my attitude toward money, but I also think I've been able to keep my feet on the ground. Running this business has taught me the value of a dollar. So I think I'll enjoy the rewards as much as anybody.

Q: What motivates you to make money?
KENNY: I think that money for me, again, goes back to keeping score. I think I'm more turned on by the deals, but, you know, again, money is a terrific way to keep track of your success. We live in America, and the business section is bigger than the sports section!

Q: As it relates to your understanding of money, Kenny, what do you think is the most important thing that you learned about yourself?

KENNY: I learned that Kenny Dichter likes money, but it's not the most important thing for me. If I had my choice whether to be playing pro basketball or have all the money in the world, I'd probably want to play pro basketball.

Q: You played point guard for Wisconsin at one point, right?

KENNY: I would say I played point guard for John F. Kennedy High School.

Q: OK. Almost played point guard . . .
KENNY: Exactly.

Q: You were on the bench as point guard, right?

KENNY: There you go. Bob, since we're on that basketball thing . . . I realized that the money for me wasn't in sports. It was in doing the other things. For me there's no better feeling than when you're out with eight people for dinner, and you just pick up the check and say, "I've got it, let's go." That's what really turns me on! Is that money? I don't know. But for me it's better than jamming a basketball!

CHAPTER 17

Sale Days

Joyce Rubin

DR. JOYCE RUBIN, 41, is an internist who resides in a Philadelphia suburb. She is married with three children: eight, six, and three.

▼

Q: Joyce, what is your earliest memory of money?
JOYCE: I guess when I was growing up. My parents were very frugal. I remember going into a store and seeing something, but always getting the cheapest thing no matter what it was.

Q: And that was your first recollection of money?
JOYCE: I don't remember anything earlier. When I was very young I didn't really pay attention to my parents buying things.

Q: What was your family's attitude to money?
JOYCE: As I said, they were very frugal. One of their principles was to always live at the least of your means. You know, don't indulge! If there were two possible things to buy, you always get the cheaper one even if the more expensive one is a little nicer or you like it better. Also always buy on sale and look for the best price!

Q: As you were growing up what were your thoughts about money?

JOYCE: Really the same.

Q: Just thinking about being as economical as possible?

JOYCE: Yes.

Q: Did you feel it was important for you to have a lot of money?

JOYCE: No. I never felt that we did not have enough. It was never that sort of thing. It was not so much we couldn't afford something as much as we shouldn't pay that much for it!

Q: Did you ever feel like you should have more?

JOYCE: No, I never felt that way. The constraints were that even for a small item that would cost 40 or 50 cents, you would be frugal even though you might have $20 in your pocket.

Q: Do you remember when you were growing up having any particular fantasies about money?

JOYCE: Never.

Q: Would you occasionally think about going into an expensive store or purchasing expensive clothing.

JOYCE: No, because it really had nothing to do with us. I didn't ever think, "Wow, if I could only have something like this!"

Q: So money was never a driving force?

JOYCE: Never.

Q: How would you characterize your current relationship with money?

JOYCE: In a way I'm not real involved with it. We have enough, and I never feel like I run through the money. My husband, who is a physician, and I make a decent living and have more than what we really need. He handles the investments. We have good investments and we have bad investments; the money comes and it goes, and I'm kind of divorced from it.

Q: Is that the way you want it?

JOYCE: In the beginning of our marriage I was more uptight about the possibility of losing money through risky investments. Now I think I'm more relaxed about it.

Q: What has made you more relaxed?

JOYCE: The fact that we somehow have more and that, in general, that attitude is better for our marriage.

Q: To what extent do you feel others judge you by how much money you have or that you find yourself judging yourself?

JOYCE: I don't judge myself at all by how much we have, but I guess other people do. I think people assume I'm a doctor and I must have all this money. We have a large house, although in our neighborhood it's like everybody else's. If someone from outside comes and sees it, it can be imposing. So I guess, you know, when people see it they think, "Wow, big expensive house!" Occasionally when people have come over, who we didn't really know—like parents of a child my kids were playing with—they've expressed amazement or awe or whatever. Maybe awe is too strong a word, but it is obvious they were impressed. Actually that makes me feel a little awkward.

Q: That makes you feel awkward?
JOYCE: Yes.

Q: What about that makes you feel awkward? That people are impressed with something that you have?

JOYCE: Right. That all of a sudden they're looking at me as a rich person.

Q: What is it about that that makes you feel uncomfortable?
JOYCE: I don't know. I always think of myself as just plain folks.

Q: So do you think if somebody is impressed with something that you have that it somehow detracts from them seeing you as just a regular person?

JOYCE: Yes. And it's not my intent to be showy.

Q: Do you make a conscious effort to be modest?

JOYCE: Not so much. A big materialistic thing in this country is a fancy car. For reasons of frugality, we don't have that. Recently we did buy a new car, but we got a good deal on it. It's a minivan and a very practical vehicle for a family of five.

Q: I get the impression that you feel like you have to apologize for the money that you have. Is that accurate?

JOYCE: Yes.

Q: Why is that?

JOYCE: I think it has to do with not being perceived as plain folks as I said earlier, or as somehow being seen as arrogant, or that the other person—for reasons of their own—might resent it. Maybe that's also part of it.

Q: So it's more of a concern about what other people think?

JOYCE: Yes. I mean, that's just my psyche, rightly or wrongly.

Q: What is most valuable to you in your life?

JOYCE: My family. You know, my husband and kids and that's really it. I mean in terms of money we have things that cost a lot: a house and the new car. But I don't think of them as things that are valuable in my life.

Q: So the money, excuse the pun, is something that's material but in a sense it's really not all that material to your life.

JOYCE: Right. I mean if all of a sudden the money in my money market account went down $10,000: let's say the bank made a mistake. It wouldn't change my day-to-day life at all.

Q: Joyce, how has being a physician shaped or affected your concept of money? I'm assuming that you must see people who are stressed by money. People who need a particular procedure and lack the ability to afford it. And of course you must see elderly patients. . . .

JOYCE: I treat a lot of people, not necessarily just the elderly. The bulk of my patients are blue-collar people. People who don't have a lot of money and who are trying to pay their bills. I don't know all the details but I suspect many of them overextend themselves. I wonder to myself that if they're short of money, why do they need to pay $30 a month for cable TV? To me it doesn't make sense. But that's my value system, not theirs.

I see a lot of people who worry month to month if they're going to be able to pay their bills. That's very far away from where I am. Has it affected me? I'm not sure, because I usually don't see people who can't afford their medical care. The nature of my medical practice is that my patients have insurance coverage. We don't see the really poor or those who have medical assistance, like welfare coverage, for example.

Q: Joyce, what about the fact that as a physician you are close to life-and-death decisions in the lives of your patients?

JOYCE: I'm not as close to life and death as you think. But I mean you're right. I do have an appreciation for the role and importance of money in the context of the larger concerns in a person's life. Really what's important is your relationships with the people who are closest to you in your life. If you're dying or they're dying, money may make a few things easier. But it's not really the important thing at all.

Q: So would you say that the fact that you are a doctor has minimized the overall importance of money in your life?

JOYCE: I've never really thought of it in money terms. However, being a doctor, if anything, has shown me the opposite. It has shown me a more materialistic and wealthier side of society. But to get back to your question, Bob, if what I've experienced as a doctor—seeing suffering and such—has made me appreciate non-material things . . . I don't think so. My practice just hasn't worked that way.

Q: Why do you think that is?

JOYCE: My patients are not usually dealing with difficult medical situations on a regular basis. You know if somebody has chronic high blood pressure, chronic diabetes, they're not thinking about life and death on a day-to-day basis. Or maybe I don't identify with them as much. Perhaps that's part of it.

Q: Is it that you're not thinking about large philosophical questions?

JOYCE: Generally I don't.

Q: To what extent do you think money has significantly affected the quality of your life?

JOYCE: Although I don't think about it, I guess it has affected the quality of my life a lot because I know most Americans worry about money. I never do! In fact, I have this sort of huge absence of worry. And I'm not aware of it. It's not like I used to worry about money and now I don't. I never really have. So I guess having enough has been very nice.

Q: Joyce, what do you think is the ultimate purpose of money?

JOYCE: Obviously beyond the basic needs, putting it away for later. For your retirement, for your kids for when they're older, and just saving it I guess.

Q: I suppose the savings must give you a great sense of psychological security to know that it is there when you need it. Is that true?

JOYCE: You know, it's not like I sit and look at the money market account statements and say, "I have so much." It is a nice feeling. I mean, I tend to put a lot of money away in IRAs and mutual funds. It is nice to look at that big balance, but I don't do it very often. The only other thing that I thought of recently related to Steven Spielberg, who obviously has a lot of money. He established this oral history thing. He videotapes Holocaust survivors talking about their experiences. You know, he funded this. This did affect me. And I realized if I had a lot of money, I mean this is not just being comfortable, I could do something important with my money.

Q: Is this something that you would want to do?
JOYCE: Theoretically, yes. I mean, I don't quite see myself making millions—being able to do something of that magnitude.

Q: But I mean do you see putting your money at its current level to use to help other people?
JOYCE: Oh yes. Very much so. I mean we do. I mean I don't know for sure what other people give to charity, but it is important to us.

Q: As it relates to your understanding of money, Joyce, what do you think is the most important thing that you've learned about yourself?
JOYCE: I don't know. Maybe nothing. The only thing is, I guess I was more uptight about investments and losing and that kind of thing. And now I'm much more divorced from it. My attitude is much more "easy come, easy go." I don't even know what's happening. I mean that's really more a function of my marriage in that my husband is involved in that. Even when we lose oodles of money, somehow we always seem to have enough. He makes it back. One year we made a lot of money in the stock market and the next year we lost it; it doesn't seem to ever be a problem. So basically I don't deal with it. And I guess if I looked at negative figures all the time, that would cause a lot of marital problems. So in a way it's really more of a marriage thing than a money thing. I want to say one more thing about money. When I'm buying things, I'm

always looking at price and wondering should I buy or should I not buy something. Even with small things, I go on little guilt trips. I think to myself, "No, I won't get this, it's too expensive." And I don't!

Q: Like what?

JOYCE: Recently, I bought a new down coat. It was on sale, of course! It was at the end of the season and I really didn't need a coat because my old one was still good. It's true that the zipper didn't work and it broke when I was still pregnant and my daughter is now almost four. I couldn't really justify a new coat even though I really wanted it. I've actually never done that before for something so expensive.

Q: How much was it?

JOYCE: It was $119 reduced from $200. But it was really an incredible down coat. And the way I justified it to myself was that I really needed a warm coat. I just get too cold and I have a problem with the circulation in my hands. So I really could use those warm sleeves. And that was my justification. It's really crazy in a way because on the one hand I don't really care that maybe $10,000 was lost in the stock market, but I have a hard time dealing with the decision to buy a $119 coat.

Q: Why do you think that is?

JOYCE: I guess if I got too upset about the $10,000 in the market, I'd get divorced. So why should I get upset? Neither event really affects my lifestyle, but the purchase of the coat is still tangible.

Q: What do you think would happen if you just went in and bought that down coat because you liked it, even if it was not on sale?

JOYCE: Like a coat that I didn't need and I just went out and bought it?

Q: It happens all the time.

JOYCE: I just can't. I may want it, but buying it is different.

Q: But you can afford it.

JOYCE: I can't justify that!

Q: Why is that?

JOYCE: I mean, you can't just go out and spend all your money! Apparently there are people who do but I don't understand that. It's very foreign to me.

Q: Why is that concept so foreign?

JOYCE: I guess it's the frugality thing. You know my parents grew up during the Depression, and I guess here it is in me. I mean here we have oodles of money. We live in a 3,200-square-foot home and until a year ago I was still clipping supermarket coupons. Finally, I just stopped because it takes a lot of time and it isn't really that cost-effective. But old habits die hard, even when you want a warm coat.

CHAPTER 18

Drilling for Dollars

Earl Augspurger

DR. EARL AUGSPURGER, 61, is an orthodontist residing in Norfolk, Nebraska.

Q: What is your earliest memory of money?
EARL: I believe my earliest memory is from the fourth grade when I started my first job.

Q: What was it?
EARL: I used to sell greeting cards door-to-door in my neighborhood. I had an old black suitcase—a fairly good-sized one—filled mainly with Christmas cards. I believe they sold for a dollar a box. I did pretty well! In truth I think it was more a case of people feeling sorry for me than anything else.

Q: Was it a positive experience?
EARL: Very much so. It gave me a real sense of encouragement to continue. After that I had other jobs like a paper route and so on. When I was growing up my family didn't have a lot of money. When I was older I visited our old home in Illinois where my father worked for the Buick Company during the war. I couldn't believe how small it was. But when I was growing up it was certainly ade-

quate. My family was comfortable: my dad made a living that provided for what we thought our needs were. And so that is my earliest memories of money and the role it played in my life.

Q: What was your family's attitude toward money?

EARL: They felt they never had enough money. It was always a point of stress in our house—worrying about how to make ends meet. My dad instilled in me from the time I was a boy to make sure I "get security." That's why from an early age I felt that I needed a strong education.

Q: Do you think this was due to the fact that he had experienced the Depression?

EARL: Yes, that's right. There were some very hard times. I was born in 1936. I was a Depression baby. As I was growing up, the Depression was still very fresh in my family's mind.

Q: Earl, do you recall any early thoughts or fantasies that you had about money?

EARL: Yes. I decided I would invest my time and money in an education. And so I got my degree in engineering. My first job was with AT&T and I was selected for their management training program. My goal was to become the president of AT&T. I figured that one person in our group would attain that position and there would be nine vertical promotions.

Q: When did you give up your goal to be president of AT&T?

EARL: I worked for AT&T for 12 years. I worked for them in Minneapolis, Des Moines, Denver, Kansas City, and New York City. When I was 30 years old I was making good money. I was in the top quartile of all the graduate engineers of my vintage, but the money was not enough. Money at that point was a great source of dissatisfaction.

Q: What do you mean?

Earl: Not enough makes you unhappy. But a lot of money or enough money makes you look at other values in life. And for me I was not able to spend enough time with my family. The money wasn't worth what I was giving up in time.

I wanted to be independent and I did not want to have to move as frequently as I had for the company, about every two years. I had a friend in high school who became a dentist who encouraged me to go into dentistry. I applied and to my surprise I was accepted to dental school when I was 33. At the age of 40 I graduated and I've been practicing orthodontics ever since.

Q: Earl, how would you characterize your current relationship with money?

Earl: Of what is truly important to me in life, Bob, I think money is about fourth down the line. I enjoy the work that I'm doing. And I enjoy the time I've been able to spend with my family. When I went to dental school, it was the first time I got to live in one place for several years and really spend a lot of time with my daughter, who was eight or nine at the time. I remember she asked me one night if I would sleep with her. Now that's the first time I'd ever been asked and I really felt that now I was a father. I'll always remember that! I just realized that there are other values that you have to have that are more important than money. Of course, money is a means of providing your family with their needs. But it's not an overriding concern. I think of other things than how much money I'm making from day to day. I love my work. I think basically it has to do with my feelings of personal achievement and I certainly don't use money as an indicator of that.

Q: Earl, what do you think is the ultimate purpose of money?

Earl: Money is a means of exchange, and you should be a good steward of it. It should be used to promote the things that you value in life. I think the ultimate purpose of money is to support a positive value system.

Q: Can you think of an important event or experience in your life where you realized the true value of money?

EARL: I think it goes back to my first job of selling those greeting cards door-to-door. At that point I could place a value on my work and my earnings. I think you develop a sense of value that comes when you are involved in working very hard at something. I think that when you put something of yourself forward to achieve money, that is when you find out what is the value of your efforts and what you are made of as a person.

Q: Earl, what do you think is the most important thing that you learned about yourself as it relates to your attitude about money?

EARL: I think the opportunities in the United States to earn money are fabulous. If you have a goal and you have the desire to be a high achiever, you will be able to attain what you want. You must also love what you're doing. If you don't, the money won't be enough. That's what I discovered about myself: that my values in life were a much higher priority than my net worth. I think I can say that what's unique about me is that I was willing to go back to school at the age of 33 and start all over again. To put all my assets on hold because of what I valued most: to be with my family and to be independent. Also to do something that helps others. I've always known money is important, but there's much more to a good life than making money!

CHAPTER 19

Mutual Funds

Carole Ober

DR. CAROLE OBER, a geneticist, is an associate professor at the University of Chicago.

▼

Q: What is your earliest memory of money?

CAROLE: You know, believe it or not, I have absolutely no memories of money. I really don't have a single one that I can think of.

Q: When did you first become conscious that there was such a thing as money?

CAROLE: I think I always knew that money existed because my parents certainly didn't mince words about what I could and couldn't have. It was also clear that lots of kids had more than I did but some had less. But truthfully, I don't ever remember thinking about money.

Q: Carole, what was your family's attitude toward money?

CAROLE: I grew up in East Meadow on Long Island in New York. My family was comfortable in the least sense of the word. We lived in a nice house and I certainly never wanted for anything. But there wasn't a lot of extra fluff. Also I always had the sense that my father was working very hard to give us this life.

Q: So, how would you characterize your family's attitude toward money?

CAROLE: Well, my parents would never talk about money with us. It was always like money was no one's business other than their business, which could well be why I didn't think about it much. They always sent us to sleepaway camp, and I always knew that was a stretch for them. But they felt it was important. And the same thing for college. They made sure we could go to college anywhere we wanted. My sister and I both went to a private college although we knew it was a struggle. My father probably took out a loan for our education, although he would never talk about it!

Q: As you were growing up, do you remember having any thoughts or fantasies about money? Did it occupy your thoughts at all?

CAROLE: I don't think it did.

Q: Do you think that's unusual, now, as we're talking about it?

CAROLE: I think it is unusual. I was telling this to my daughter, Jill, and she couldn't believe it. Jill certainly has lots of thoughts about money all the time!

Q: So how do you make sense of that as we're talking about it now?

CAROLE: I don't know. I think it's partly due to the fact that my parents never spoke to us about money. And I don't think that personally I ever wanted a lot of things. So I didn't fantasize about material things.

Q: Do you think it's more a case of denial or one of indifference?

Carole: It feels like indifference, because I never felt deprived of anything. So if I really wanted something, I can't ever remember not getting it if I really wanted it badly.

Q: How would you characterize your current relationship with money?

Carole: Complete indifference. It drives my husband crazy.

Q: Could you elaborate?

Carole: Money, to me, is a very abstract concept. I just don't have a good sense of savings and planning for the future. I also don't have a particularly good sense of what we can and can't afford.

Q: It's just not something you think about?

Carole: Exactly. It's not something I think about and it's not something I really grasp that well, even when we talk about it. Although I might understand money on an intellectual level, it just doesn't seem to be particularly meaningful.

Q: There's no strong visceral connection?

Carole: That's right.

Q: How does your husband react to that?

Carole: Well, he finds it very frustrating, because he is much more conservative about money. He is much more focused on investing and making sure that our future is well taken care of. He would much rather sacrifice on a day-to-day basis to have this future thing. In truth, it's just something that's very hard for me to understand.

Q: What is your response to his point of view?

Carole: I can understand why it might be important, and I might appreciate it someday, but it seems to me more important to live in the present.

Q: Is this a tension that's easily resolved?

CAROLE: Yes, simply because I don't care that much about it. I suppose if I really cared, it would be more of a tension.

Q: To what extent do you feel that others define you by how much money you have, and to what extent do you ever feel that you use that as a yardstick for self-definition?

CAROLE: Bob, I think the major thing that attracted me to academia is that people aren't valued by money, other than, of course, the grant situation. When I was growing up, my father worked in the garment industry. I grew up in an extremely materialistic world. We belonged to country clubs and I experienced the whole Long Island thing! I always felt extremely uncomfortable in that whole environment. When I started graduate school, I felt as though I had found my own world because no one cared about what you wore. Nobody cared how much money you had or where you lived. In fact, the more odd you were, the better!

Q: You found a world away from the materialism?

CAROLE: Right. Of course, I think there are people in academia who probably do judge people by how much money they have and are impressed by wealth. But I think that for the most part it's a nonissue. But the grant issue I don't think is so much about how much money you have but rather how much clout you have, or how much influence. It seems to be very important to have those large dollar amounts after your name. I must say that I've only benefited from that. Again, as it relates to money, I'd have to say it's something that I just haven't thought much about.

Q: So you haven't thought about it, but you've been able to generate the grants?

CAROLE: Yes. And it's clear to me that the way people view me at the university is based on the fact that I bring in a lot of money. That's a little disappointing, but it's very true. And you can be doing outstanding research, and if you don't have the grants to back it up, somehow there's that doubt about the work—that it may not really be that important.

Q: Have you ever attempted to deal with that issue head on?

CAROLE: I think it's well known. I think people know that is just the way the university works.

Q: Do they talk about it?

CAROLE: Not a lot, but it comes up in promotion committees. And it comes up when you're talking to the faculty about your expectations. But the way the current situation is in terms of the economics of running a university, it's a hard problem to overcome. It's not about personal gain, so perhaps that's why it seems so different to me.

Q: But it still is all about money.

CAROLE: Yes, absolutely!

Q: Carole, could we talk a little bit about your research. You have lived with and studied the Hutterites over a long period of time. They are a religious group of people with money and materialism almost absent from their culture. Could you relate what that experience has been like?

CAROLE: Bob, first let me tell you something about them. The Hutterites are an Anabaptist religious group, which means they believe in adult baptism. The other Anabaptists are the Mennonites and the Amish. These three groups were formed during the Protestant Reformation in Europe. The Hutterites come from the Swiss-German area of the Alps. In addition to believing in adult baptism, the Hutterites differentiated themselves from the other Anabaptists by a belief in a communal lifestyle. As far as I know, they're the most successful communal group in the New World and perhaps in the whole world. About 800 Hutterites originally came to the U.S. and there's now about 35,000 to 40,000 in the U.S. and Canada, all descendants of that original group. They are quite inbred and there have been virtually no new members in the community since they first came to the United States. Although they do have people leaving the community, it's proportionately a fairly small number.

Q: Did you study one community or more than one?

CAROLE: I've been to about 32 of their communities. My first trip to visit the Hutterites was in 1983. Because my main research is on fertility, I usually work with the married women. It's just very neat to see that the newly married women are the little girls that I knew 13 or 14 years ago, so I feel like I've personally known two generations.

Q: Could you talk about the Hutterite world, specifically how it relates to material concerns and how it distinguishes itself from contemporary American culture.

CAROLE: It's really very interesting. The Hutterites have very large families that live on these huge farms. And they believe in modern technology, so a lot of the farms now are computerized. But they have no private ownership. There's no concept of individual wealth. Each community has a treasurer who controls the funds. And all profits go into a central account. Each family receives a small allowance that they can use if they go into town and they want to buy things. But in general, mostly everything that they own is bought in bulk by the community. So each home looks almost identical to every other home. If the colony decides that everybody should have a cuckoo clock on their wall, every house will have the same cuckoo clock! So central to their belief system is to do away with individuality. Accordingly, they will dress alike, and they will own everything alike. It's interesting though because there are a few areas where they don't have to buy in bulk and they get to express how kind of wild their tastes are! They wear eyeglasses, which they buy individually, that are truly incredible with wild geometric patterns.

Q: So they use their eyeglasses as a way of distinguishing themselves?

CAROLE: I think so. They wouldn't say that, but certainly when you look at them, that is your perception. Also their shoes. They don't buy shoes in bulk. So they wear all sorts of sneakers. They're all different colors and some have glitter things on the back. So when they walk, it's like lights going on and off. And the adults and elders wear them, too.

Q: They have no concept of individual ownership?

CAROLE: It's much more than that, but it's hard to describe. For example, they know that they will be cared for throughout their lives. There's an enormous sense of security among the Hutterites to the point where they're not even aware of it because they don't know any other way. This is something that I'm certainly aware of when I'm there. So anyone who gets sick, or anyone who can no longer contribute to the community, is cared for by the other members. There is no sense of worrying about the future, worrying about anything that's related to money or finances!

I personally think that they have something that is wonderful that we could never have on the outside and that is that they never have to take money into account. As a community, they do; but as individuals, they don't. On the other hand, they give up a lot for that kind of security.

Q: Do you think it's worth it?

CAROLE: Well, I think unless you're born into it, you could never do it. I don't think it would be possible for anyone who hasn't been raised as a Hutterite to live that uniform an existence. I remember once having a conversation with a young man about money. It was interesting because he couldn't understand why anyone who had a job and made a salary couldn't buy a home. And I was trying to explain to him that houses on the outside are very expensive and that a lot of people on their salaries could never make enough money to buy a house. He could not understand that. He just looked at me in disbelief!

Q: Well, of course, it was completely foreign to his experience.

CAROLE: I guess that they have the view that if you make a personal salary, you can buy whatever you want.

Q: What would you say the Hutterite community most values?

CAROLE: I think community first and foremost. Unlike other Christian sects that believe in salvation through the self, the Hutterites believe in salvation through the community. You sacrifice your own individuality for what's best for the community. And although that might sound unpleasant at certain levels, at times of crisis or need, it's really an invaluable resource to them. I have seen some pretty bad accidents in the colony. I think that might be fairly typical of many farming communities. There was a fire a few years ago that killed six children in one house and you could see how the community came together. The depth of support that they offer one another is really something to envy.

Q: Carole, to what extent do you think your experience with the Hutterites has shaped or affected your personal understanding of the value of money?

CAROLE: I don't know if it has directly impacted on my thoughts about money as much as my thoughts about what's important in life. I think I really value relationships with people. I'm not sure if I learned that directly from them or it's just something that has become crystallized in living and working with them and observing how completely sincere they are in the things they say and do.

It's very unusual to be with people who are totally nonjudgmental. It almost throws you off guard. And you don't realize how unusual that is until you are in these communities. You can be with people, who truly see you for who you are, not because you have material goods or a Ph.D. When I'm with them they say there's real doctors and there's Carole! They wouldn't know anything about grant money, nothing! And they just like me, because they know I like them, and I enjoy being with them. It's just so completely different from what you experience in your everyday life. I think it has just made me realize how important are the relationships with my family and friends.

Q: Carole, as it relates to your understanding of money, what is the most important thing that you learned about yourself?

CAROLE: I think again primarily how important relationships are. You look around at our culture and you see the materialism. It has become a pretty American characteristic. I mean, it's almost as though people think they're entitled to so much. And I don't know what it stems from, what psychological aspect of our culture has given rise to that, but it's really disturbing. Also, for so many people their wealth and their possessions are what they feel defines them. I think it comes from their insecurity. They think their wealth makes people look up to them. They have a big house and think people say, "Wow, that must be a really important or neat person." It is quite sad that a lot of people define themselves in this way. To me it seems like a very shallow existence.

CHAPTER 20

The Pursuit of Purpose
Abraham Twerski

DR. ABRAHAM TWERSKI, 63, is medical director emeritus and founder of the Gateway Rehabilitation Center and associate professor of psychiatry, University of Pittsburgh School of Medicine. Prior to being a psychiatrist, he was a rabbi in Milwaukee for ten years. He has authored more than 20 books on wide-ranging subjects involving issues of religion and personal values.

Q: Dr. Twerski, what is your earliest memory of money?

DR. TWERSKI: My earliest memory of money is that of stories that I heard from my father about the concept of *zedakah,* the Jewish concept of charity. And the tradition in the family was that money was something to be given away, rather than to keep. The family stories that we heard—I won't say day in and day out, but quite frequently—were how our ancestors, all of whom the last ten generations were rabbis, would receive money from donations and contributions from their followers—sometimes huge donations— and they lived in almost abject poverty because whatever they received, they would give away.

Q: So as you were growing up, the attitude that was imparted to you was that the purpose of money was to serve others; not for personal use or gain but rather to have a social purpose?

DR. TWERSKI: Right. There was almost a guilt about keeping money!

Q: Can you elaborate on that?

DR. TWERSKI: Well, it comes from several reasons. First of all, we must remember that all of this took place in the old country where there was no welfare system and people who were poor had no safety net. If they did not receive charity, they starved and had no place to live. There was something there that is completely different from what we refer to as poverty in the United States, which is perfectly compatible with owning an automobile and a television set.

Q: Where did you grow up?
DR. TWERSKI: In Milwaukee.

Q: How did your family's attitude toward money impact on you directly?

DR. TWERSKI: From the very beginning I looked at possessing and saving money as being wrong from two aspects. First of all, if others needed it, what right did you have to keep it in the bank? Secondly, if you really had belief and trust that God would take care of you, then you earn enough for today and place your trust in God for tomorrow. The attitude was whatever you absolutely didn't need today for necessities, give away.

Q: How would you characterize your current relationship with money? Is it consistent with that attitude?

DR. TWERSKI: Consistent in this way: in no way do I approach the kind of attitude toward charity that my ancestors had, although I wish I did. But that would aim me for perfection, and I don't deceive myself that I could do that. However, there has remained a very difficult weak spot in that I have found it extremely difficult to charge adequately for my services. People in my capacity provide a service for a fee and have a much higher charge and a much higher income than I have had.

Q: You mean as a psychiatrist?
Dr. Twerski: Right.

Q: So how have you been able to resolve that?
Dr. Twerski: I resolved it by remaining on essentially a salaried position. In that way I don't have to say to anyone, "Pay me for what I do for you."

Q: And that was a conscious effort on your part not to work on a fee-for-service basis?
Dr. Twerski: Right, completely conscious, because I knew where it would go.

Q: In your universe of values, Dr. Twerski, what do you think is the ultimate purpose of money?
Dr. Twerski: The purpose of money is simply to have enough for one's necessities. One must define "necessities" as real necessities rather than when luxuries are defined as necessities. Let me tell you one of my favorite stories. An individual once came to a psychiatrist.

The psychiatrist asked, "What is your problem?"

The man said, "I have no problems."

The psychiatrist rejoined, "Then why are you here?"

He answered, "My family said I had to come."

The doctor looked at him and asked, "What do they think is wrong with you?"

The man quickly answered, "They think that there's something wrong with me because I love pancakes."

And the doctor said, "Well, that's the most absurd thing I ever heard. I love pancakes, too."

"Oh, you do!" perked up the man. "Then you must come to my home. I have trunks that are full of them!"

Now, the moral of the story is that making four pancakes for breakfast is fine and putting them in the freezer for the next day is fine, too. But when you start treating them as though they are an end in themselves, that's absurd. That's the way I look at money. When it has a reasonable purpose, fine. When it becomes an end in itself, it's as ridiculous as collecting pancakes. However, American culture does not see it that way, and so people who have more than enough money for themselves and for their children are still pursuing money when they might be doing something more worthwhile with their lives.

Q: Dr. Twerski, your clinic practice has centered on working with addictive personalities, and I was wondering from your perspectives what are the implications for people who accumulate money. Is it fair to say that some people do accumulate money addictively?

DR. TWERSKI: Of course. I think of the addictions to drugs and alcohol as just one. There's also addiction to food, addiction to fame, addiction to power, and addiction to making money. And that's what I believe was revealed when they asked J. Paul Getty how much is enough, and he said, "Just a little more." That's exactly what the alcoholic and heroin addicts feel—they must have just a little more.

Q: To what extent do you think money has significantly affected the quality of your life?

DR. TWERSKI: Well, I believe that I have not been immune to wanting things that were not necessities, and I have deviated from the ancestral attitude toward getting along with bare necessities. So I'm afraid that I have pursued, even though I have never been wealthy, more than I actually needed, and that has deterred me from fulfilling myself in the spiritual sense. I think it has had a negative effect.

THE PURSUIT OF PURPOSE

Q: Dr. Twerski, what is your response to the contemporary culture that we all live in, where there is such an emphasis on consumerism and materialism, speculation and investment?

DR. TWERSKI: Well, it's pretty much exemplified by the story of the pancakes. I see the world, Western civilization, for many reasons as sinking up to its eyeballs in hedonism. What has happened is we've misinterpreted "pursuit of happiness" to mean "pursuit of pleasure." There's been a major revolution in the past several decades as a result of medical science and various technological advances that have led people to think that being free of distress and having ultimate pleasure is an attainable goal and should be the inalienable right of every individual. And I think also what has happened is that young people have picked up on this and realized that if this is the goal of the adult world, it can also become the goal of 11- and 12-year-olds. But since they cannot achieve the kinds of things that adults do, they have implemented this pursuit by the use of drugs. I think that the consequence of the hedonistic environment we're living in is that every year the age of onset of drug use becomes lower. We now have marijuana beginning at age 11, and the epidemic of drug use among young people increases annually in its severity.

Q: Dr. Twerski, what is most valuable to you?

DR. TWERSKI: Immediately most valuable is my religious beliefs and my feeling of purpose in life. I'm not quite there yet! Of course, also my family—my wife, my children, my grandchildren.

Q: Can you think of any particular personal event or experience where you felt that you suddenly recognized the ultimate purpose of money in your life?

DR. TWERSKI: No, I don't think so. I cannot think of any single event that stands out. But as I mentioned before, it has been an ongoing belief and experience with the ideology of *zedakah* that I have been speaking about, that has been repeated so many times over that it became part of me.

Q: How has being both a rabbi and a psychiatrist shaped your concept of money?

Dr. Twerski: You see, being a rabbi in itself does not make a person immune to the impact of American culture. Not even being a Hasidic adherent protects, because unfortunately, some people have been able to reconcile contemporary values with their alleged adoption of Torah and Hasidic values. In actuality, the two are really in gross conflict with one another. And it's unfortunate that this has occurred. So my concept of money is not so much from being a rabbi as from the ideology that I was taught.

Q: So then being a rabbi, in particular, didn't affect or shape the way you internalized the concept of money.

Dr. Twerski: Right. Because, look, we have rabbis driving around in Lexuses and Cadillacs; it had nothing to do with the profession of rabbi.

Being a psychiatrist had perhaps a more profound effect, because I was brought face-to-face with clients. I had some patients who I treated who had more money than they knew what to do with. And this did not stop them from experiencing severe depression, total despair, suicide, whatever. I treated families whose money was really the source of the downfall of their children. They became irresponsible, even drug addicted. Certainly, as a psychiatrist I began to see the fallacy of the pursuit of money even more than I did as a rabbi.

Q: What do you think it is about money that hangs up American society so?

Dr. Twerski: There is a feeling that money provides security. For many people there is a feeling of insecurity that has perhaps various sources, but people see their salvation in money. People see their acquisition of love and friendship in money. In many of my writings I have focused on the problem of low self-esteem whereby many people have unwarranted feelings of inadequacy and inferiority. People with those problems are particularly prone to feel that they are unloved and they do not trust that other people like them, even their own families. And they, therefore, feel that they must acquire money in order to be able to buy friendship or to buy love. For example, I was seeing a couple where the husband was an excellent provider. After the youngest child was old enough to go to school, the wife had time available, and she took a course in real estate and obtained a real estate license. After she began making money, the marriage almost fell apart. And the reason for that became very evident as we saw the couple, because the husband did not feel that he was capable of being loved. His security in the marriage was that his wife would need his economic support, hence she would not leave him. When she began to earn on her own, he felt terribly threatened. To him money was the way he was going to retain his wife's love. For many other people—even people who are philanthropists, people who are doing wonderful things—they feel that their money will buy them into the good graces of others, and it does.

Q: What about our emphasis on material goods?

DR. TWERSKI: Well, again, it depends on what one sees as one's goals in life. I think that even people who claim to have a religious orientation nevertheless feel that this world is the one existence that they have. They want to get the most that they can out of it: "eat, drink, and be merry, for tomorrow you die!" A religious belief says that reward does not come in this world. There is an afterlife, where you get your ultimate reward, and the function of your existence in this world is to do God's will, which is primarily to do good for others, rather than to be primarily egocentric.

I think that true value is something that has to be inbred from early training. It's based on an ideological system that a child is taught, which is totally different than the prevailing value system.

Q: As it relates to your own understanding of money and value, what do you think was the most important thing that Abraham Twerski learned about himself?

DR. TWERSKI: I again restate the fact that I grew up with the feeling that money is not to be hoarded, that once you provide for your necessities, you make it available to others. The favorite story that my father used to tell was of his grandfather, a Hasidic rabbi who despite a very large following never had enough money for his family's household needs. When grandmother would say that she needed money for the household expenses, he always said he didn't have it. One time, a wealthy follower from Kiev visited, and grandmother knew that this person would give a handsome contribution. As soon as the man left, she went into the study and said to grandfather that she needed money for expenses. His reply was, "I'm sorry. I don't have any." To which she said, "How can you say you don't have any? The man certainly must have given you a handsome donation." "Yes," he said, "but look, I have two pockets. In my right pocket is the money for the household expenses. In my left pocket is the money for charity." He continued, "What can I do? The money the visitor gave me went into the other pocket; it's not mine!" To her protests, he finally said, "Look. The Almighty has a system. He did not distribute wealth equally. He gave some more and some less. And then appointed some others to try to equalize it a little bit." He continued, "I'm one of the appointees, where I'm supposed to try and take what the wealthy have and make it available to the poor; that's my job. Because I'm performing my job well, I have the right to keep a small commission for myself. If I should take more than a small amount for myself, it's going to be embezzlement and I'll soon lose my job and then we'll have nothing!" That was the kind of attitude with which I grew up.

Q: So what you've most learned about yourself is that . . .

DR. TWERSKI: I wrote about this in one of my books. I was one of the people who, without having any good reason for it, grew up with feelings of inadequacy and inferiority. And many things that I used to do early in life were to try and compensate for those feelings. At age 38, a group of events brought me face-to-face with a realization that I was down on myself and I began looking better at myself and developed a totally different picture. So what money could have meant to me, had I not grown up with my particular orientation, was a source of security. I never got quite to it, because it was discouraged. But what it meant for me in personal terms was a very negative self until I was almost 40.

Q: Dr. Twerski, are you trying to say that what you learned about yourself was that you could develop a feeling of security within yourself as opposed to finding it in external things?

Dr. Twerski: Exactly.

CHAPTER 21

Stocks and Ponds

David Held

MR. DAVID HELD, 35, is a member of the International Monetary Market where he is a Eurodollar broker and professional speculator.

Q: What is your earliest memory of money?
DAVID: My earliest memories of money have to do with my birthdays when I was young. I would get cards with money in them from my relatives, you know, my grandma, grandpa, whoever. That was my earliest introduction to money. I came from a big family and money was tight when I was young. My parents raised six children, each of whom was one year apart. My dad was the only breadwinner in the family and my mother did not speak English.

Q: Where was she from?
DAVID: Both my parents are from Germany. My dad came over in 1958 and my mom came over in 1959. They were already married before they emigrated, but my dad came over first to find work in his trade. He was a carpenter.

Q: And you are one of six children?
DAVID: Yes. I'm the third child.

Q: David, what was your family's attitude toward money?

DAVID: Money was very tight with us and so if you needed something, a shirt, a pair of shoes . . . if your older brother was outgrowing them, that was your new pair of shoes. It was hand-me-downs, basically. But if I was going to a big party or something special, I would get a new garment. But in general, money was scarce and my parents believed in being thrifty and made their money stretch as far as possible.

Q: As you were growing up, what were your thoughts about money?

DAVID: I really didn't think much about money until my dad finally told me one day that if I really wanted something I should go out and get a job!

Q: How old were you?
DAVID: I was 11. I got my first paper route.

Q: What did you learn from that experience?

DAVID: I learned that if I really wanted something I had to go out and get it myself. No one was going to hand it to me. I didn't come from money, so if I wanted something, it would be up to me to provide for myself.

Q: Did you feel money was an important thing to have?

DAVID: Absolutely. When you are one of six you appreciate things more.

Q: And you felt having a job provided you with new opportunities?

DAVID: Yes, not only making money but also meeting interesting people.

Q: Do you remember having any particular fantasies about money?

DAVID: Yes. Absolutely. My total fantasy when I was young was to have enough money to buy a fishing resort and retire there and relax.

Q: And just fish all the time?

DAVID: Yes. My younger brother, Peter, and I would talk about that as we were growing up. It was kind of our ultimate dream.

Q: Is it still one of your dreams?

DAVID: It is. As a matter of fact, I just bought a house on a lake—so I'm halfway there!

Q: So you're living your childhood fantasy, in a way?

DAVID: I would have to say in a way I am!

Q: David, do you believe money is either the root of all evil or the sum of all blessings?

DAVID: I think it's both. As the saying goes, "Money makes the world go 'round." It won't buy you happiness, but it will get you a hell of a good time. At the exchange you can really see how different people's attitudes are toward money just by observing their behaviors. One guy wants to hit the home run right away. I'm more conservative. I'm going to make $500 or $1,000 each day and I'm happy.

Q: You're trying to hit singles?

DAVID: Yes. I'm not interested in putting everything on the line like some people. I don't want to get the overnight phone call that the Singapore market just tanked and I'm wiped out!

Q: How would you describe your current attitude toward money?

DAVID: My current attitude is the same as when I was younger. I believe nothing is given to you free, you must go out and earn it. You must save your money and invest it wisely. I'd never go out and be frivolous. I'm not the kind of person who says, "Oh, I want that 52-inch color screen TV. I can't live without it!"

Q: Do you find you make a conscious effort to do without?

DAVID: Yes, absolutely. I can afford many things I choose not to purchase. I think it all goes back to my childhood. Again, I learned early on that nothing is handed to you. You have to work hard for what you get and money is not to be frittered away.

Q: That's pretty much been your life theme?

DAVID: Yes, because it works! No one is going to hand you anything in this world free of charge.

Q: David, to what extent do you feel others define you in terms of how much money you have?

DAVID: I really don't consider it all that important what other people think about me. It's not an issue. I think the best description I could give of myself is a blue-collar worker inhabiting a white-collar world. People probably say about me that "he knows what he's doing and he doesn't pull any punches." Frankly, I don't think money really comes into it.

Q: What do you think is the ultimate purpose of money?

DAVID: I think just to have enough, not to be extravagant. I mean, I can afford to buy a Jaguar, but I choose to drive a Saturn. My brother works for GM. He told me it was a good, reliable car, so I bought it. I like knowing that I can go out and buy my fishing resort or I can just sit on my money. I've always been impressed with a guy like Sam Walton. The man had so much money, but he chose to drive a beat-up Ford pickup truck. He did not flaunt his money, either. Now there's a man I can emulate! You know he did not live in the biggest house or was extravagant with his money, even though he was worth billions.

Q: And that's pretty much your attitude. Is that correct?

DAVID: Yes. I'm going to be happy with whatever God throws me.

Q: As it relates to your understanding of money, what do you think is the most important thing that you learned about yourself?

DAVID: That's a tough question. The most important thing that I learned about myself is that I'm a patient person. Like I said earlier, I'm conservative with my money. I could put all my money in the stock market, but I don't. Instead, I put it into U.S. savings bonds and the like where I know I'm going to get a guaranteed return. I'm just basically the same person I was when I was younger: hardworking and basic.

CHAPTER 22

Pocket Change

Tom Cummins

MR. TOM CUMMINS, 48, is an art historian specializing in pre-Columbian and colonial Latin American art. He has lived and worked in Latin America.

Q: Tom, what is your earliest memory of money?

TOM: I remember once being at the dinner table with my grandfather, who was a banker. I said, "Oh, I'd love to see a brand new crisp dollar bill." I don't know why I said this, but I remember him suddenly producing and handing me a brand new bill.

Q: How old were you?

TOM: I must have been four or five. He didn't have a wallet. He took it out of a billfold, so the money had never even been doubled.

Q: What were your thoughts at the time, do you recall?

TOM: I couldn't believe that he did that. It really was the idea of the fetish of a dollar. I mean I wasn't going to spend it. We lived out in the country and there wasn't even a store I could go to. It was just having it!

Q: Tom, was it the fascination of possessing some magical substance?

Tom: Yes. Very much so.

Q: Do you think that in any way your fascination with art and artifacts is related to that experience? Were you sort of drawn to the artistic aspect of the bill?

Tom: No, I don't think what appealed to me was the artistic elements, although one could say that I became fascinated with its meaning. The idea of something—a dollar. The same kinds of things that I work with today: the idea of representation and the idea that people will enter into a symbolic world and conduct all kinds of social interactions has continued to occupy my interest.

Q: Tom, are you saying that your fascination with that dollar bill is consistent with your interests now?

Tom: Yes. I think that's right. Of course I wouldn't have known it then, and after that I was never really interested in money. I grew up in a privileged world where everybody had money, but you never saw money. People would get this thrill from having money, but wouldn't display it. It was just a very typical WASP attitude. For example, you would have a station wagon, but the idea that someone would drive a Rolls Royce was really tacky.

The other thing is that although money wasn't displayed, it was always there. You know there were vacations and houses on Martha's Vineyard or Sea Island, but the money per se was not displayed. When I think about it now, it's clear to me that the money definitely was thought about. I mean, it was extreme luxury. You would go skiing in Europe and spend summers in Nantucket. In comparison to others we didn't have that much, but most of the people we knew had a tremendous amount of money. It was just a very different world. I really didn't know anybody who didn't have money, except for the people who worked for us.

Q: Do you remember your family expressing any particular attitude about money as you were growing up, or was it more just the ambience and the background that you just described?

Tom: It was more that. I went to boarding school where everybody certainly had a lot of money. But the important point, Bob, is they didn't talk about it. Nobody ever talked about money!

Q: Does that seem odd to you?

Tom: Well, no, it doesn't. I think it seems odder to people who didn't grow up in those circumstances. It's very hard to explain to people what it is to grow up in a life of privilege. In a sense it's a very isolated existence.

Q: Tom, how would you characterize your current experience with money?

Tom: I would say that I made a very conscious decision that money was something I was not going to pursue; that is, I found no value in it for its own sake and it was something I was not interested in. I went to Wall Street to work in a bond trading room. I found it to be so mundane! Completely empty. I was trading huge quantities of money, to the point that it was totally unreal in terms of my own existence. At the same time, I couldn't hold a decent conversation with the other traders. The idea of spending the rest of my life doing this convinced me that I would either go brain dead or become an alcoholic! I mean all these people made tons of money: $50 million, $60 million, $100 million.

Q: It never interested you to accumulate money?
Tom: No.

Q: How old were you when you began working on Wall Street?
Tom: I was 21.

Q: And you knew right away it wasn't for you.

Tom: Exactly. I mean, it was all fair to me, it was all very easy. But you see, Bob, that was what I was expected to do. I was to go into Uncle Andy's firm and earn my fortune. He owned a beautiful old building on Pine Street, where everybody made a lot of money.

Q: Do you ever regret that you didn't take advantage of that opportunity?

Tom: Not for a second. But there were a few interesting moments, like the time I went out for a drink with $30 million in bearer bonds in my back pocket.

Q: What?

Tom: My uncle asked me to carry $30 million or $40 million in bearer bonds to the Federal Reserve Bank. Ex-cop Quinn, who used to carry a gun, accompanied me so we could put the money on deposit. You know how it works? So we went down to the Federal Reserve and for some reason, the window was closed. So Quinn turns to me and says, "OK Tommy, me boy, let's go for a drink." So we walked into a bar, and I'm sitting there, drinking beer, with $30 million in my back pocket. Needless to say, I was feeling very uncomfortable! Quinn obviously sensed my discomfort and said, "Never mind, Tommy. There's at least 20 guns in the room!"

Q: You know, Tom, there are not many people in the world who've had the experience of walking into a bar with $30 million in their pocket. I guess if the bartender knew you were carrying that kind of money, he would have bought the first round.

Let me ask you another question. You have a very interesting career. You've lived with indigenous people throughout Latin America. Could you talk a little bit about how that experience has shaped your attitude toward value and money?

Tom: You know, Bob, there's several ways to answer that. Some of them are anecdotal. For example, I remember being in Lima, Peru, in 1990 and experiencing the hyperinflation and what that does to the value of money. The currency was constantly readjusted and people didn't know what anything was worth. You couldn't buy anything because people had no concept of value. And I remember the only things you could buy were U.S. dollars. I mean almost everything in the economy came to a standstill. There wasn't even prostitution! No material desire could be fulfilled. Nothing was changing—except money.

Q: Dollars.

Tom: Yes. People wanted dollars, because it was a currency that was stable, so the idea was to accumulate dollars. You couldn't even get a cab! It was very strange. I had to go to Cusco and I finally found a place where I could change some money. The person who was running the money exchange said to me, "Look, I must get some money to Cusco. I will drive you to the airport if you will deliver this envelope." It was $10,000 or $15,000 that he had to get to his partner. There was just this tone of absolute desperation. The idea of trusting somebody you've never met before with $15,000 to get onto a plane and carry money.

Q: What did you learn from that experience?

Tom: I learned to recognize the face of absolute despair. It was an experience that I was in many ways outside of because I was not seriously physically or materially threatened by it. And yet I was deeply affected watching people who were just stunned at what was happening to them. Fortunes evaporated overnight.

Q: What about the day-to-day living conditions?

Tom: Well, what's incredible is people can go on! I mean, people do manage to cope. But the infrastructure was shut down. There were no stoplights and there was no electricity in the city.

Q: So the whole economy came to a halt.

Tom: Yes. And the people who had some money had generators. But the whole pulse of the city literally changed. You could hear the throbbing in the streets of these small generators. It was pretty bizarre. But the essential experience is something that my son Ian articulated when he was about six when we were living in Ecuador. I'll never forget it. He came home one day, and said, "You know, Dad, here we're very rich, but in the United States, we're not!" He understood the idea of relational value, the relativity of wealth. When you live in these situations you appreciate how many people really live in dire poverty. I mean, some of our friends were really living in conditions that are quite extraordinary.

Q: What do you think you've learned from these experiences?

Tom: Bob, I believe I've developed a certain attitude. I mean we're living right now in a boom time. But conditions could be reversed very easily. I think that I am better ready for a downturn than most people. I understand that that can happen. I also understand, I believe, how to reprioritize exactly what it is that you need to live.

Q: Tom, what is your personal perception of the stock market frenzy that we're currently experiencing?

Tom: I think it's a real time bomb. I mean, I don't know how you feel about it, but to me it's like a giant Ponzi scheme, and ultimately people are going to get caught.

Q: What would you say is most valuable to you?

Tom: My time. I mean, that's all you have. You have a life, and you have to choose what it is you want to do with it. If I want to dedicate it toward the acquisition of material goods, that's one alternative. Personally, I've found that to be not very intellectually stimulating.

Q: As it relates to the whole issue of money and value, what do you feel you've most learned about yourself?

Tom: It is an interesting question, but I don't think an easy one to answer. I was lucky from the start because I was in a position at a young age to decide what I wanted to do. And I really had it all. I feel fortunate to have had the opportunity to choose a career that really interested me, whereas the easier decision would have been to go to work on Wall Street. I mean, as I worked through graduate school and ultimately decided what it was I wanted to do, I slowly came to trust my own decisions. I developed a confidence in the decisions that were intuitive. I don't care what anybody says—rational choice be damned! The ones that come from your heart are the most important.

Q: So what you learned was . . .

TOM: . . . to trust myself about money and everything else.

CHAPTER 23

Personal Finance

Howard Abell

MR. HOWARD ABELL, 56, heads an institutional investment division of Rand Financial Services. He is the author of three books on personal finance. He is a principal of Tao Partners.

▼

Q: What is your earliest memory of money?
HOWARD: My earliest memory of money is tied to my family's business. My mother and father owned a fish store where they worked together.

Q: Did you work there when you were a boy?
HOWARD: Yes, absolutely. During summer vacations and school holidays and other times when it was very busy my brother and I were drafted to help out.

Q: Your family encouraged you to help out?
HOWARD: Of course. And you actually learned the value of a dollar by experiencing the hard work and effort that it takes to accumulate money.

Q: What was your family's attitude toward money?

HOWARD: That it was something that you had to work hard for and that it was something that allowed you to live as comfortably as possible. There wasn't an enormous amount of money, but what there was was used to live a middle-class lifestyle.

Q: As you were growing up, Howard, what were your thoughts about money? Did you feel it was important for you to have a lot of money?

HOWARD: I thought that I would like to have a lot of money because I felt that I wanted to have at least the lifestyle of my family, which was essentially middle class in New York City. However, I also had ideas of bettering that because there were some relatives in my family who were at higher income levels.

Q: Did you take any specific actions to make money?

HOWARD: No. For various reasons I became a teacher. My background was in education, and I taught for two years but was very dissatisfied. I felt I was stuck in a box. I felt there was no upside potential for me materially.

Q: How would you characterize your current relationship with money?

HOWARD: It's a love-hate relationship. I think that I've always placed money in what I believe is a healthy context. I'm not one who is interested in accumulating vast sums of money for its own sake. Of course, I still value money for the lifestyle that it can and has afforded me. It has enabled me to do some of the things that most people want to do: the leisure time available to spend with my family and to pursue other interesting choices.

Q: Howard, you work in an industry that has been characterized as the last bastion of free enterprise. I know you have observed individuals who have accumulated—overnight—vast fortunes. Some have kept them, but most have not. What's your overall observation about that?

HOWARD: I have seen both the rags-to-riches and riches-to-rags scenarios take place in this industry. More often than not, I am reminded of the adage, "A fool and his money are soon parted." I believe that for the most part, people seek a level in terms of their psychological ability to handle money. So if somebody comes into a financial industry like this one, where money is available because of a temporary circumstance—a bull market for example—and the money that is made is not attributable to any fundamental individual ability, then in many instances, the money soon disappears. It's similar to what you see with lottery winners where people who have never had money win huge sums of money. Psychologically something happens and their lives are not better off for having the large sum of money. They're more dissatisfied in their lives than people would ever imagine!

Q: In what sense do you think they're dissatisfied?

HOWARD: They can't cope with the money psychologically. They haven't been brought up to understand money and they realize that the lifestyles that they're used to and that they want to live have little to do with money. And so their psychological expectations interfere with enjoying the money. It interferes with their lifestyles. People who have grown up at a particular social level find that they have no more friends at that level. And they don't have the ability to make friends at a higher level.

Q: Howard, are you saying that the introduction of money into the lives of these people exacerbates other problems that they're already experiencing in their lives?

HOWARD: Absolutely. You know there is always a Henny Youngman joke about money that illustrates a point.

Q: Can you think of one?

HOWARD: I'll have to paraphrase it. There is the one about the man who comes running home and announces breathlessly to his wife, "Won the lottery! Won the lottery!" He's packing his bags and his wife says, "Fabulous. Where are we going?" And he says, "What do you mean, *we!*" If you study the lives of people who win lotteries or people who have made vast sums of money overnight, their domestic lives in many instances are torn apart.

Q: To what extent do you feel others define you—either positively or negatively—in terms of how much money you have?

HOWARD: Well, I think whatever I might feel comes from within, not from outside myself.

Q: Do you define yourself in terms of how much money you have?

HOWARD: I don't define myself in terms of how much money I have. I do define myself more in terms of the lifestyle I am leading and how it is an outward sign of accomplishment. And that accomplishment coming in a very difficult industry is even sweeter.

Q: More psychologically satisfying?

HOWARD: Yes. It isn't the amount of money, it is the idea that I have the ability to be successful where most people aren't. So the trappings of that success just become a sign that "I have arrived."

Q: A sign to yourself or to the outside world?

HOWARD: More to myself, actually. I was never really ostentatious about money. I live well, but I've given up German luxury cars and extraordinarily expensive vacations for other things that are more interesting.

Q: But it was important for you to do that, right?

HOWARD: It was important.

Q: What would you say is the most valuable thing in your life now?

HOWARD: I think what's most valuable is psychological security and having the time to pursue my personal interests. To travel and read and to have the time to explore new ideas and relationships with my friends and family.

Q: Howard, what do you think is the ultimate purpose of money?

HOWARD: I think it goes back to the beginning. I think the ultimate purpose of money for me is to establish a lifestyle that is good and rewarding for me. It's secure and it allows me to do the things that I want to do. And that includes working. I think the contemporary concept of retirement is a fallacy.

Q: To what extent do you think money has significantly affected your quality of life?

HOWARD: Well it's just the trappings of what money can buy, the comfort level. Psychologically it is a way to keep score that you had accomplished some things that were difficult and that you're successful. For me there was never the intensity to try to accumulate enormous sums of money.

Q: How has working in a financial industry shaped or affected your concept of money?

HOWARD: In the roaring late '70s and '80s, it was easy to get caught up in the frenzy of the marketplace. There was easy money and substantial sums came and went. And luckily in my case came and stayed. As I look back it was easy to get caught up in that and watch others around you get caught up in just the electricity of that period.

Q: Can you think of a particular event or experience where you felt you had a better appreciation of the true value of money?

HOWARD: There are a lot of little events. For example, there was a time when I was going through a particularly rough period in the market. I had lost a lot of money through one or a series of trades. In an attempt to shore up my emotional state, and also to put my losses in perspective, my wife—who was also a trader—demanded that we go out to the fanciest restaurant in Chicago at that time, Maxim de Paris, and we did. My son, my wife, and I had an extraordinary dinner and spent more money than most people would want to spend. And all at a time when things were going downhill.

Q: What did that dinner accomplish for you?

HOWARD: Well it said a couple of things. It put everything in perspective, that we weren't going into debt to pay for this dinner. We were a viable entity. It also gave us a boost to remember that we were still in good shape. It was a spirit lifter and then we went home and said, "Now we have to focus in on what we know we can do so we can pay for this elaborate meal!" It was kind of a joke. And as things turned out, it was near the bottom of the trough.

Q: Howard, what is it about money that hangs people up so?

HOWARD: I think it has to do with the fact that money is a means to a lot of different things. It's not only a means to comfort, it's a means to status, it's a means to power, and it's a means to psychological comfort. It's almost like a drug in the affects that it can have on one's psychological and emotional well-being. I think in that sense money can be very chemical and an agent that fosters dependency. I think that it's possible that money may very well induce a biochemical reaction in the brain similar to a drug.

Q: As it relates to your understanding of money, what do you think is the most important thing that you learned about yourself?

HOWARD: I think it goes back to the idea that money was there to testify to the fact that I had success at something that I attempted to do, in what I thought was a very difficult area. I guess it's what we used to say was a way of keeping score. Really what it did was indicate that you had proven success. I think that people who are doing things that don't bring them a lot of money find indications of success in terms of specific intellectual or physical accomplishments that are just as important. So for them, the motivation is less monetary. I guess what I learned about myself is that I need both!

CHAPTER 24

Making Too Much Money

Steve Franklin

MR. STEVE FRANKLIN, 53, is a reporter for the *Chicago Tribune*. His assignments have been diverse, ranging from investigative reporter to foreign correspondent to labor writer, which he has been doing for the past seven years.

Q: Steve, what is your earliest memory of money?

STEVE: I don't really have a good early memory of money or of spending it. My family was relatively poor and didn't have a lot of money. The only thing that I do recall is the people who had money.

Q: What do you recall about that?

STEVE: The fact that somebody may have had an expensive car or a larger apartment or went on vacations. My father was a postal worker who worked nights in New York City and my mother worked part-time in a clothing store. My parents divorced when I was young and I was sent to live with my father. I spent most of my time by myself, and money to me was simply not that important. I didn't feel I didn't have it, but I noticed that others did.

Q: As you were growing up, do you remember any particular thoughts or fantasies that revolved around money?

STEVE: No. I never truly had great ambitions to have money. I felt it wasn't important, and from an early period on—I waited 'til I was six to decide what career I would pursue—I knew I'd be a writer. So money was never an important issue for me. In fact, the first three newspaper jobs I was hired at, I never even asked how much they paid and I never asked for a pay raise because I felt that I liked the work so much, and it was so important, that questions about money were not material.

Q: The idea is that your source of satisfaction came from the writing, not from the money. Is that it?

STEVE: Right. The money didn't matter.

Q: Do you recall your father having any particular attitude about money?

STEVE: No.

Q: Money was not something you ever spoke about at home?

STEVE: No. There wasn't a lot but there was no grief or despair or great concern about it. It was a simple assumption—this was all, this is what we had. What I did feel as a youngster was that poor people were discriminated against. They were not understood, and what I didn't understand was why. I couldn't understand why poor people were not given as much of a break or understanding. I mean, money clearly affected my life. The way I chose a college I remember was to look up the three colleges in the United States at the bottom of the list based on cost. Those were the ones I applied to.

Q: The three private schools that cost the least amount of money?

STEVE: Right, but that didn't bother me.

Q: What were they?

STEVE: I think one was Bradley and the other was Drake and there was another one that I forget. I wound up going to Drake University in Des Moines, Iowa. I only stayed there for a year, and then I transferred to Penn State.

Q: How would you characterize your current experience with money?

STEVE: Well, I think I've become very middle class, and I'm conflicted about it. There are times when I think I make too much money. I still have the same feeling that if the newspaper ever knew how much I liked what I did, they'd make me pay them money for it.

Q: Would you?

STEVE: I would. I mean, there are moments—usually when I'm working overseas—that are so rapturous and so exciting and I just feel so much in sync with what I'm doing that I can't believe I'm getting paid money for it.

Q: Steve, the idea of evaluating yourself in terms of how much money you have—is that a foreign notion for you?

STEVE: Yes. Practically speaking, money was never a factor. But I've also been a bad manager of money. For years I refused to buy a home because I didn't think it was important to invest in a house. I think we were one of the last couples in our age group who bought a house. We became money managers by default, because having children required that we take into consideration our expenses. However, we're still terrible at it!

But, you know, I don't feel bad about it. I think that I've always had a career where money wasn't the most important thing, so I've taken risks and made changes. I think I'm a risk taker, and I think another person in a similar situation wouldn't have done the things that I did. I'll give you an example. I was on strike in Pittsburgh on a newspaper, and I was out of work for five or six months. My wife had given birth to our daughter, and we had exactly $200. We cleaned out our savings account, and I was getting $35 a week strike pay. I was also selling locally articles for $5 and $10. I wanted to go to work for the *Miami Herald*, which was interested in me, but it didn't have an available job. They told me in fact, "you can't come down." Nevertheless I took all the money we had in the bank and bought an airline ticket to see them. I got there, and they said, "Well, we're glad you came down. But why'd you come down?" I told them, "I really want to work for the *Herald*. I'm not making any money and I want a job." Then I explained to them I'd taken the last penny I had to fly down to see them.

Q: Did you get the job?

STEVE: Yes I did. I guess my feeling was what else could they do?

Q: Steve, what do you most value?

STEVE: The things that I most value are things that you can't hold or touch or look at. It's events, experiences, relationships. It's having encounters. These are the things that I most enjoy. There's nothing that I value where I truly feel the need to say I own this or I own that. Yes, my wife and I collect art, and we do like to acquire, but I could easily give it all away. After college, Suzanne and I joined the Peace Corps. I think that experience taught us about living with people and doing things. It gave us the sense that acquiring is not as important as being an inquiring person.

Q: Steve, to what extent do you think money has significantly affected the quality of your life?

STEVE: Oh, as we have more money our oriental rug collection gets bigger, and occasionally we get better rugs. These are things that provide connections for us because we've spent so much time in the Middle East. (Steve was a Peace Corps volunteer in Turkey and a Middle East correspondent.) But again, money for us has never been critical. And when we don't have money, that's never been a problem either.

Q: Steve, you were the Middle East correspondent for the *Chicago Tribune* and now are the labor reporter. You also write feature articles. You have, in my opinion, a very rare sensitivity for people who live in conditions of poverty and affliction. Could you talk a little bit about that and how that has formed your overall concept of value?

STEVE: Bob, like I said, we were not rich. My father was a postal worker who didn't make a lot of money. I was shocked when I discovered that people actually had bedrooms. I thought that most children lived in and slept in the living room when they grew up. As I mentioned, my mom divorced my dad when I was young. She moved to Puerto Rico and then came back, and in the last years of her life lived in public housing. She sold hot dogs at the racetrack in New York City. Seeing her in that condition always touched me. And I didn't think she was any different than most people. It was her indecisiveness that made her poor, condemned her in a way. And I think, if anything, that gave me a great sensitivity to understanding those situations.

When I worked in the Peace Corps in Turkey, I learned to respect poor people and the beauty and humbleness of them. When we lived in Istanbul we ran an orphanage where we worked with the Istanbul police. We also worked with people who had terrible backgrounds but who were able to overcome their troubles. After the Peace Corps, I worked in the New Jersey prisons, in a juvenile reform school, until I was 26. I was the admissions officer, and who did we admit? Poor people. People who, as far as I could figure out—these were youngsters between the ages of 8 and 11 years old—simply had been born in poor situations. So I have all of those experiences to guide me. I think journalists by nature are iconoclastic; we tend to have a passion for the underdog. And I think when I came along in newspapers, one of the great joys of newspapering from the '60s onward was speaking out for people and having the ability to level things whenever possible. I don't think that exists today. I don't see the passion, the fury, the fire in the stomachs of journalists. Maybe it's because they're better trained, they're not alcoholics, they're not bizarre, they're not deranged, as some of them were in the past. But journalism, big-city newspapering, engenders this whole fixation on what's going wrong with the system. And so for years I spent time writing about poor people in many different ways: as victims of crime, lacking adequate housing, being denied good jobs. Probably what propelled me into writing about these things was that other folks didn't like it. Besides, like a jockey, I've discovered I'm good at riding certain horses!

Q: Steve, as you look at America in 1998 and see the blatant materialism everywhere, what is your personal response?

STEVE: I find it very difficult to relate to, and I found it was a great shock returning to America at the end of 1990. I was stunned by how much people have here and how easy things were to acquire. I don't like it and I don't feel comfortable with it. I do have to add one thing though. I'm astounded at how good my living is. I never knew journalists could be treated so decently. And I think if the word was spread widely, they'd take it away and keep us in chains. It's one of the perverse truths of society that social workers and public health workers and teachers are paid so poorly while the private sector pays well. Now I don't make a lot compared to a 27-year-old who's great with computer graphics, but I make a damn good salary. I often wonder about my priorities there. I wonder whether I'm doing enough. I also feel I have the need to share. For a number of years I taught at Columbia College here in Chicago. I figured out I really made no money teaching, but it was something I wanted to do and something I felt it was important to share.

Q: As it relates to your understanding of money, Steve, what do you think is the most important thing that you learned about yourself?

STEVE: That's an impossible question, because I can't relate to it the way you posed the question. There's no sign, cosign, or tangent to indicate that I'm part of that equation that relates to me and money, because money for me has not been the driving issue. If anything, it's been the opposite. Money for me is just the ability to do things.

I was very much affected by Albert Camus in the sense that I believe my true value is a measure of my value to every other person, and that because of the often bizarre nature of the world I live in there is no obvious consistency in what I do. My value is how good a person I am to everyone around me and how good I represent myself. When we first moved to Turkey, I was struck by the obituaries in the Turkish newspapers. They never said what the person did for a living in the first paragraph. In Ameria we would never do that. The Turks are more interested in honor and personal integrity. I think what I learned from the Middle East is the importance of knowing who you are as a person. That true value is the ultimate measure of your dignity and personal character.

CHAPTER 25

Count Me In

Michele Carbone

Dr. Michele Carbone, 35, is the director of the Laboratory of Molecular Virology and Oncology at Loyola Medical Center. He is a leading authority on how viruses cause cancer.

▼

Q: Michele, what is your earliest memory of money?
Michele: I don't think I have one.

Q: You don't have an early memory of money?
Michele: No.

Q: When was the first time you became conscious of the fact that there was such a thing as money?
Michele: Well, maybe my father used to give me the equivalent of 50 cents every time I got ten 10s. In Italy you scored from 1 to 10 in school. So when I got ten 10s I would get 50 cents.

Q: Could you talk a little bit about your family's background and their attitude toward money?
Michele: My father is an orthopedic surgeon. He has practiced orthopedics for 37 years. And my father's family is all doctors. I am the seventh generation of doctors. And my father is very careful

with his money. He doesn't like to spend money and he doesn't like to risk money. He's not going to buy anything that is risky. He doesn't buy stocks. Federal government bonds, yes, but no equities. My mother is the opposite. She's a diplomat, or I should say she used to be. She thinks that money is close to being a bad thing and simply not something that one should worry about.

Q: Close to a bad thing?
MICHELE: Yes.

Q: But not something that one should worry about?
MICHELE: No.

Q: You also come from a fairly privileged background. Is that correct?
MICHELE: We have never had money problems.

Q: You actually have a formal title, is that right?
MICHELE: What do you mean?

Q: An aristocratic title?
MICHELE: Oh, you mean whether we are counts? Yes. But I have never really cared for this thing and I've never been very much interested in it.

Q: You're not interested in it but it's part of your family heritage.
MICHELE: The last one in my family who was interested in this thing was my grandfather.

Q: What was his title?
MICHELE: I can't remember, really. I've never cared about that stuff.

Q: Michele, how would you characterize your current attitude toward money?

MICHELE: My attitude toward money changed when I left Italy because America is a different country. My attitude about money changed primarily due to the fact that in the United States everything is valued in terms of money. I think though that maybe my attitude overall is somewhere in between my father's and my mother's.

Q: Could you explain in terms of your approach toward money?

MICHELE: I definitely don't think that money is bad. I think that it is a good thing to have. I don't value people based on their money. It is my observation in the U.S. that people are valued mostly by the amount of money they have. I've lived in the U.S. now for 12 years. My first response was that this behavior was uneducated and rude. In Italy the attitude is much different. Where I come from if you are rich, you don't say you are rich so as not to embarrass the people around you. Here I've met many people who will tell me, even after meeting them for just a few minutes, what their paycheck is. It is unbelievable, unheard of! People will tell me, "I make $500 an hour." Who cares? I think it is very tacky, rude, and offensive.

Q: What is your response to the emphasis on consumerism and materialism?

MICHELE: Bob, I really don't know. This is a great country. There are a lot of things that you can buy. In order to buy them you need money. And it seems that in America there is an endless amount of things that you can buy. And because it's endless people always want more money. On the other hand, it's not that you're buying bad things. You buy positive things. You buy a nice car. You buy a nice house. You buy nice clothes. So it's not that the money is used in a bad way. What offends me is the obnoxious attitude of flashing money in the face of people who may not have money. And the smug attitude of some people who may have millions of dollars in the bank. The way I grew up is that you don't value people for their accounts at the bank. People are valued for who and what they are. It has nothing to do with the money.

Q: Michele, in your professional life you are concerned with issues of life and death. How has that affected the importance that you place on money?

MICHELE: I don't think it has. But I see that people try to accumulate huge sums of money and then they die. It all seems stupid! I mean they work so much to accumulate wealth and before they can enjoy it they suddenly die. In my work, I see people who die just like that! Unexpectedly. So it doesn't make much sense . . .

Q: To spend your life accumulating money?

MICHELE: Yes, you exert all this effort to accumulate money, for what? So maybe to answer your question, Bob, this does affect my personal attitude toward money and what is really valuable.

Q: Michele, what is most valuable to you in life?

MICHELE: People and relationships. A friend I can trust. Somebody who is not there because he thinks that he can get something out of me because I'm a famous scientist. I like to be around people who are authentic and genuine, who understand what are the essential elements of a good life.

Q: To what extent do you find yourself personally using someone's response to money as a test of their character?

MICHELE: Well if I don't like a person's attitude toward money, I don't want them to be my friend. So in that sense, I do. I don't like people who spend their lives just accumulating money or things. So my response is that I don't want to deal with them.

Q: You don't want to be associated with them?

MICHELE: No, people who are acquisitive—or for that matter people who are cheap, who always say they can't spend $5 because they forgot their wallets at home when it's clearly intentional—I find that very tiresome.

Q: As you think about the whole issue of money, what do you think you most learned about yourself?

MICHELE: The money is important but it has never been a motivating force in my life. Of course a lot of it had to do with my family background. I came from a family that has money. I wouldn't say we are billionaires, but clearly I knew I would never end up in the street starving. I have chosen to live modestly. I like to do certain things and in order to do them I have to be able to pay the bills. So there is no doubt that I have to have an amount of money that allows me to do what I like to do. So that comes to a point that I need to earn that money. But not to make money for the pleasure of accumulating it. It's unclear to me why people do this. After you've accumulated so much, what the hell are you going to do with it?

CHAPTER 26

No Shortcuts
Paul Ciolino

MR. PAUL CIOLINO, 41, is a private investigator. He has worked on high-profile criminal investigations for 17 years, including the O.J. Simpson and JonBenet Ramsey cases.

Q: What is your earliest memory of money?

PAUL: I suppose it would be getting an allowance as a young child.

Q: For doing chores around the house?

PAUL: Exactly. Doing chores around the house, helping my mother, taking out the garbage, washing the dishes, that sort of thing. I come from a very humble background. My dad was a car salesman and my mom was a full-time stay-at-home mom. And let me tell you, we lived from week to week.

Q: As you were growing up, what was your family's attitude toward money?

PAUL: Very blue collar. Be honest. Pay your bills then you eat. Only then can you buy something with the leftover. Most of the time there was no leftover! In fact, you're lucky if you were eating!

Q: Are you saying, Paul, that when you were growing up your family was living paycheck to paycheck?

PAUL: Yeah, pretty much. We always had a small home. For my dad, that was the dream. I mean, that house was it.

Q: Do you remember having any particular thoughts or fantasies about money?

PAUL: I can tell you that my earliest and most repetitive fantasy was, if I could make $500 a week I'd have it made! That would be it. I'd have achieved success beyond my wildest beliefs. I thought then I could own my own home and probably have a car. Maybe even be able to go on vacation once or twice a year. So for me that was the ticket!

Q: So you've done that. What does "it" feel like now?

PAUL: Obviously the scenario has changed a little bit. Now if I could make $40,000 or $50,000 a week I'd be really happy. Actually, Bob, my financial success has gone beyond my wildest dreams. If my father were alive, he'd throw up at some of the things I spend money on. I mean he would just look at me and say, "What are you doing?"

Q: Like what, for instance?

PAUL: Well, like a Rolex watch or something of that nature. He'd just wonder why you'd need a $12,000 Rolex when you could buy a $15 Timex. I mean, both tell time! I buy $1,500 suits. I mean, never less than $1,000. And that's when they're on sale. Or a custom-made shirt. That was unheard of for him. He had one pair of brown shoes, one pair of black shoes. I've got 17 pairs of shoes at $200 apiece. For my dad, it was $20 apiece and you'd resole them until they fell apart.

Q: So having said that, Paul, how would you characterize your current relationship with money?

PAUL: Well, that's something I never really thought about. I'll tell you, for the most part it's a necessary evil. Got to have it!

You've got to make it and there's only one way to do it. That's in an honest and forthright way. I've learned one thing, there are no shortcuts!

Q: Well, let's talk about shortcuts because in your business you were involved in the O. J. Simpson investigation in Chicago?
PAUL: Yes.

Q: You've been a commentator on CNN for the Cunanen and Ramsey cases. What have you learned from these experiences?
PAUL: I do a lot of fraud investigations, both for corporations and private individuals. Mostly people, you know, doing accounting... monthly check statement comes in and oops, we're missing $270,000 and where is it? And invariably it will be a trusted longtime employee. They might be skimming the pennies or nickels and dimes off of the paychecks every month for two years and all of a sudden they have $260,000 saved up. There is one case that I was working on where an accountant was stealing from his partners. They were just starting up and couldn't figure out why they were losing money all the time. One partner kept saying, "We should do an audit." And the accountant said, "No, we don't need no damn audit. We're barely making money, we can't afford no audit!" Well, finally the partners prevail and they do an audit and sure enough, the accountant skimmed off $300,000. Of course he was doing the books, so no one ever double-checked. And they were lifelong friends! It was just another shortcut. He thought he was smarter than all of them. He thought he should be making more money. It's just classic. The typical shortcut. It just never ceases to amaze me that people would do that to friends, family, and relatives because it always blows up.

Q: So in your experience, when people take shortcuts they generally get caught?
PAUL: Almost always. And you know why? Without exception, they steal for luxury items! Never for necessities—never for the

mortgage, never for the absolute car payment they have to make so they can get to work, never for medical bills. To hell with the medical bills, they can wait, right?

Never to feed the children. It's always for the BMW, the boat, the drug habit, the gambling debt. It's never for anything substantial or for a necessity.

Q: It's really interesting that you point that out because when I interviewed Matt Mahoney he said exactly the same thing about people who murder for money. In his experience it's rarely out of desperation. Usually it's out of greed and self-centeredness to acquire a bigger home or car or something like that.

PAUL: Yeah. Well murder is always in my experience a result of love, sex, or revenge. You can almost always get rid of every other motive besides those three. And with one of those three, usually, you find out who did it!

Q: Paul, let's go back to what you were talking about a moment ago. In your experience, people take shortcuts to get luxury items.

PAUL: Almost always.

Q: And why do you think that is?

PAUL: I think most people believe themselves to be more talented and brighter than they are. Or they are dissatisfied with what they've achieved so far in their lives. And they always feel that they're being held back by somebody or something. That it's never their fault, it's always someone else's fault.

Q: A victim's mentality?

PAUL: Exactly. I'm a victim, therefore it's OK if I steal from you. I'll give you a perfect example in the financial markets. At the board of trade, for instance. You have people making millions of dollars. But you also have runners and clerks who are working on the floor. And people who are typing and transcribing prices. They look at you and sometimes say, "I'm as smart as him. I should be making that kind of money, too!" And they're in a position to hurt or steal from you. Their attitude is, he's made so much, he'll never miss it. And I deserve it 'cause I'm such a great employee! I work so hard and he doesn't even recognize what I'm doing. I'm going to get it one way or the other. And if I don't get caught, great. And if I do get caught nobody will probably say anything anyway!

Q: What has been your observation of their attitude when caught?

PAUL: Unapologetic. You know what I'm saying, Bob?

Q: Right, because they justify the crime.

PAUL: They have to. They have to justify it 'cause if they have any measure of conscience they wouldn't be able to deal with it.

Q: So it's their way of getting even. Is that right?

PAUL: Yes, however with one big "but." They never get even because of course they get caught and they lose their jobs. And now they're really desperate. You see, in reality they just end up compounding the problems they already have in their lives.

Q: Paul, let's change gears. You work all over the world with some very wealthy clients. Is that correct?

PAUL: Yes. That's right. I have superwealthy clients. I've literally worked for the wealthiest man in the world, the Prince of Brunei. It's interesting to see the different levels of wealth because there are significant differences. When I was younger, I never knew that. Rich was rich. I didn't distinguish.

Q: What was your personal perception of the wealthiest man in the world?

PAUL: It's play money at that level. I had never seen anything like it before. Bear in mind I have worked for some very wealthy people.

His estate is basically in the middle of the jungle. You really don't realize what wealth is until you see the vastness and depth of what the money bought. Airplane hangers filled with luxury planes. Private jets with solid-gold bathroom fixtures. Floors and walls with gold inlaid just because he can afford to have it.

Q: Were you impressed?

PAUL: No, oddly enough I wasn't. I'm not impressed by that kind of wealth. I found it kind of scary, maybe even a little boring. I don't think I'd want that kind of responsibility.

Q: Paul, how do you think your career has shaped or affected your attitude toward money?

PAUL: I was talking about that very thing at lunch just the other day. I had a near-death experience three years ago this Easter.

Q: What happened?

PAUL: I took a muscle relaxer. I used to have a chronic bad back. And after I'd play golf, I'd take this pill. So it's Easter morning and I take the pill and within 30 minutes I'm almost dead. I'm laying there in an ambulance and all I could think about while they're shocking me with the paddles is my young children. I have four kids. I heard the doctor screaming to the paramedic that my heart stopped beating and if he doesn't get a needle in me my veins will collapse and I'm done. And I'm thinking, what a shame that I'm not going to see my kids grow up. And of course I go through all of this intensive care and I survive this and I come through fine. And I think: listen, I'm going to stop all this silliness of working six days a week, 12 hours a day, traveling around the world. From now on I'm going to pay more attention to the family. And you know, I always laugh when I hear a guy like Michael Jordan say, "I'm retiring to be with my family." The son of a bitch is on a golf course every day! He is always in Florida, Bermuda, not in Highland Park with the wife and kiddies!

So I'm really committed to being a new man and I said to myself, five days a week, I'm going to really try to get home at six o'clock every night and put the kids in bed. Within three months I was back to the old grind. And it disturbs me, but I learned a lesson.

Q: What did you learn?

PAUL: The lesson is that you can't have it both ways! You can't be this great family person and a great provider. At least I can't. I'm not that talented. I don't know how people do it. I would really like to be able to find that . . .

Q: Balance?

PAUL: I'd like to have enough money that allows that. But to make the money you've got to be out there.

Q: Paul, as it relates to the whole issue of money, what do you think you most learned about yourself?

PAUL: What I've learned is that you absolutely have to have enough money to have a nice balance in life. To provide the things I want for my children and live the standard of living that we have grown used to here in the United States. In Malaysia, living on the river, their standard of living is a lot different from ours. So I believe the money is an absolutely necessary evil that you have to have in order to function and survive. But I don't want so much of it that it would make me lazy or stupid or I'd be like some of the people I've seen. That's the bottom line! I just want enough, and truthfully I don't know where or how to reach that level. I want a vacation home. I want a boat. I don't really need a boat, but it would be nice to have one sitting out there on Lake Michigan. I don't know. You tell me. When is enough, enough?

CHAPTER 27

Making Locomotives and Money

Edward Kibblewhite

Dr. Edward Kibblewhite, 53, is a professor of astronomy at the University of Chicago.

Q: Edward, what is your earliest memory of money?

Edward: I remember my parents were quite poor. I must have been seven or eight at the time and they had to sell their house and move to a different one. I was a very inventive child and I can remember thinking that I would make an invention that would make lots of money and solve the family crisis. I think that was the first time I ever thought about money.

Q: You felt that you would come up with a terrific invention that would alleviate your family's financial crisis.

Edward: Yes. Actually, Bob, I have a slightly earlier memory. I can remember my grandfather would give me two shillings. They were big coins, which he would hand me whenever we would visit. It was an awful visit. I hated it and I used to feel that the coins were a way of buying me off.

Q: Edward, do you recall what caused your family's financial crisis?

MAKING LOCOMOTIVES AND MONEY

EDWARD: I don't actually know. My father had been a major in World War II. When the war came to an end, he found it very hard to find a job and I think he had just bought a house that was expensive and probably beyond our means.

Q: Where did you grow up?

EDWARD: I grew up in Yorkshire, in a small town.

Q: As you were growing up, do you remember having any particular thoughts about money? Is it something that occupied your thoughts?

EDWARD: No, hardly at all. I come from a culture that thought it was very vulgar to speak about money. When I was in school this idea was reinforced, so people just didn't do it.

Q: We know in English society it was also vulgar to talk about sex, but that didn't prevent people from thinking about it, so I'm wondering if the same thing was true of money for you as you were growing up?

EDWARD: I just believe that once you had your pocket money and it was sufficient, you didn't think about it. That was pretty much all there was to it.

Q: Would you say that the emphasis placed on money in the United States is greater than it is in Great Britain?

EDWARD: Absolutely. I think it is very interesting just to look at how my family dealt with monetary issues. My father made the money, but he never dealt with it. All the bills and all the hassle with money was completely handled by my mother.

Q: Have you carried on that tradition?

EDWARD: Yes, wholly. I think money is basically a dirty commodity and one should not bother with it.

Q: One shouldn't bother with it?

EDWARD: But of course that causes terrible problems.

Q: Edward, how would you characterize the difference between the English attitude toward money as contrasted to the American?

EDWARD: In England, I believe people don't look at your wallet. It's much more of a class thing. Your profession, the university you went to . . .

Q: More of one's social status?

EDWARD: That's right. When I first arrived in America, I was shocked by this emphasis on money. In London, the whole thing was how entertaining you were, whether you understood how to play the social games. If people were not able to play they were cut off. Whereas in the United States the whole thing is just much more quantitative: how much money you have determines your status.

Q: Edward, what is your current response to the American view of money?

EDWARD: Well, I think being part of this whole culture of money makes life much harder. There is this constant attitude that you shouldn't be sitting around wasting your time chewing the fat or having dinner parties. You should be out there making money! It's just much more competitive here.

Q: Competitive as it relates to . . .

EDWARD: Everything.

Q: How would you say that your profession as an astronomer has either shaped or affected your personal understanding of money?

EDWARD: To begin with, I make machines. These are very expensive machines. When I was very young and a student at Cambridge I received a large grant. Because my field is highly competitive, securing this money for research was a huge status symbol and gave me a big sense of pride. One's status in my field is based on how much money you generate for your department and your research projects.

Q: Are you saying, then, that your professional status is measured by how much money you can bring in to the university?

EDWARD: Of course, it affects your status.

Q: Edward, what is your personal reaction to having your professional status evaluated in terms of how much money you can generate for the university?

EDWARD: Well, it's a direct measure of one's worth.

Q: Yes, but how do you respond to that concept?

EDWARD: I say it's fine.

Q: You say it's fine? Do you think that's a fair evaluation of one's ability?

EDWARD: Astronomy is a highly competitive field, and I suppose it's a way of gaining brownie points.

Q: You know, John Grisham sells better than Euripides, but I would hardly consider his work as being better.

EDWARD: Well, that's right. But when you secure a large grant, there's a real buzz. . . .

Q: That you've made it?

EDWARD: Yes.

Q: Do you think that's a constant, whether it's in the United States or in England?

EDWARD: Sure.

Q: What about the idea of people in this culture evaluating their own self-worth by how much money they have?

EDWARD: Well, I find that a very strange concept!

Q: But it's one you've observed.

EDWARD: Sure. And I guess I find that really perplexing. I think I find the whole concept of money to be quite mysterious. People put money into a bank account, you can then spend it, but the whole concept of money, which translates into concepts of what you are, I find quite strange.

Q: Less mysterious than the universe?

EDWARD: I don't know. I think it's much the same. I wasn't brought up with the idea of money as a means of acquiring other things or experiences.

Q: Have you ever thought of focusing your telescope on the issue of money. Is it something that warrants your attention?

EDWARD: Well, yes. Actually, right now, it's becoming harder and harder to get grant money and so I'm thinking of setting up a company whose aim will be to make as much money as possible. I'm reminded of a quote by the poet e.e. cummings: "Poets are in competition with people who make locomotives and who make money."

Q: Are you saying that also goes for astronomers?

EDWARD: Yes. I think you decide whether you want to make things or you want to make money. I want to see what it will be like to concentrate on making money, but I know I don't have a killer instinct.

Q: But you're at a point now in your career where you feel that you want to just test the waters to see if you can make more money, is that correct?

EDWARD: Yes, because it's becoming harder and harder to make things.

Q: As you think about this whole issue of money, what do you think you've learned most about yourself?

EDWARD: I think that I've learned that I'm a very creative person who has a lot of childlike qualities. And I suppose I associate money with being grown-up. You know, money is what grown-up people have and use.

Q: It sounds like you're the Peter Pan of the astronomy department.

EDWARD: That's right. The money kind of puts you face-to-face with responsibility and adulthood, which I would like to avoid.

Q: Do you think making tons of money will provide you with the ability to be more childlike?

EDWARD: No, absolutely not. I think once you bite the apple, that's it!

CHAPTER 28

Aesthetic Values
Alan Koppel

MR. ALAN KOPPEL, 48, owns an art gallery specializing in modern masters. He is a former member of the Chicago Board of Trade and Chicago Mercantile Exchange.

▼

Q: Alan, what is your earliest memory of money?

ALAN: I actually have two. The first one is that as a child I had trouble counting, and my father taught me how to count using pocket change. That is how I developed an understanding of money and numbers and the connection between the two. It was the realization that money and numbers have a physical dimension, that money is about numbers, but it is also a material object. The second memory I have about money is quite different. I grew up in a middle-class neighborhood in Queens and I remember going with my parents to Manhattan and observing the contrast of wealth between where we lived and where the "rich people" lived. That memory stands out in my mind very dramatically. I recognized the relative value of money—the money of Park Avenue and the money of Queens.

Q: What was your family's attitude toward money?

AESTHETIC VALUES

ALAN: My family's attitude was that money was one's entrée into the American dream. They were first-generation Americans, and I believe they viewed money as a way to assimilate into the mainstream.

Q: As you were growing up, do you remember having any particular thoughts or fantasies about money?

ALAN: Yes. I wanted to be rich. I always thought that there were definite benefits to having money, and those benefits would buy me happiness, or whatever I desired. I think it was very typical of growing up in a high-achieving family of that period. I think all my educational choices also were centered around the idea of making money, having a career in something solid. So my mother would say, "You have to be a professional." It was a term that completely suggested security in financial terms.

Q: Could you elaborate?

ALAN: When I was in college I basically had a number of different majors. I kind of jumped from major to major. Remember I was in college during the '60s, living a real hippie lifestyle. I always felt that as soon as I got out of college, I was going to start a career that would give me a certain level of financial security. The first profession that I became involved in was financial and agricultural futures trading. This was 1971, and I realized that the career I had chosen was in essence the pursuit of becoming wealthy and that's how I thought about it. I was very single-minded about what I had to do. I believed money was the calibrator of success and so I was determined to become wealthy, because I wanted to be successful!

Q: Would you characterize the level of success that you feel you attained in your trading career?

ALAN: I made money from the second month I was down on the exchange floor. I mean, I refused to lose. I was convinced losing was an attitude. I realized that every day was a new ball game and winning trades bred winning trades. It also produced a certain level of confidence, which allowed me to have more winning days and greater and greater success.

Q: Do you feel then that you gratified your childhood fantasies about making a lot of money?

ALAN: Completely. I mean, I lived in the best building in Chicago with the fanciest apartment and surrounded myself with an incredible collection of art and photography.

Q: So you accomplished what your mother wanted. You had entrée to the American dream?

ALAN: The apartment I was living in was formerly owned by Robert McCormick. I mean that's traveling a pretty long distance in one generation!

Q: So, basically, all your dreams as they related to money came true.

ALAN: Yes. Except that I became incredibly depressed, because it seemed to me that all the money really went nowhere for me. It left me feeling very empty. I was completely unsatisfied. I mean, I had a great family and I absolutely fulfilled all my initial fantasies as they related to money, but I realized what I was looking for could not be secured in monetary terms. That's why I left trading. I left the exchange when I was 43. I couldn't see continuing. I felt it was a very unfulfilling life. And remember I was at the pinnacle of my career. I was good at what I did and widely recognized as being successful. And I had all the trappings of success: houses, property, cars, art—you name it! But I wasn't fulfilled.

I now believe that the reasons I felt this way was because I achieved my family's goals—meaning my parents' goals for me—but I hadn't fulfilled my own goals. Maybe I was just chasing the wrong thing to secure what I was really looking for: personal fulfillment. I felt completely unproductive. I just wasn't enjoying what I was doing and I realized I'd have to take steps to change my situation.

AESTHETIC VALUES

Q: So what steps did you take?

ALAN: I thought about doing something in a field that I really loved. It came to me in a flash: art. I had spent the past 20 years collecting and had formed a very fine personal collection. I realized I could join the skills I learned as a trader with my passion for identifying great art. The timing was perfect. The art market peaked in the late '80s, and just like any other market, there was an incredible downturn that I knew meant opportunity. I had done very well collecting in the '80s, and I felt that if you had the funds, you could purchase outstanding works. There's an old axiom in trading: "Buy low and sell high." The problem is that when you're buying low, everybody else is selling. So you really have to have a lot of conviction at that time. The same thing is true with selling high. Everybody thinks you're nuts when you're selling at the top of the market, because "they all know that the market's going higher!" Frankly, for me dealing in art requires the same analytical skills.

Q: So in essence you were able to combine your love of art with your knowledge as a trader to start a new career. Is that correct?

ALAN: Yes, I was a very active art collector, and the love of art and the idea of being in a business that involves itself with art—where I can surround myself with wonderful paintings, sculptures, furniture, and objects—is my dream come true!

Q: Alan, in what you do, what is it that you truly value?

ALAN: What I love about art has to do with the discovery. Looking at something and determining if this really has worth in terms of a stated aesthetic value and in terms of monetary value, because you're making two decisions all the time. So there is this ongoing process. I see a lot of different things, and determine if a piece is good enough for the overall collection and for my clients.

Q: Alan, the art that you specialize in is modern masters. You handle works by artists such as Picasso, Léger, Mondrian, and

Ernst—to mention but a few that I see before me. You often sell works of art in excess of a million dollars and you regularly come in contact with people who have very large financial net worths, people who can afford to spend millions of dollars on a painting. How has this affected your personal understanding of the concept of money?

ALAN: You know, the thing with well-known works of art is it just makes you sit back and think about the whole complex issue of wealth and value. When somebody buys a Picasso, it's not just about buying that work of art. It has to do with the confirmation of their wealth, and the confirmation of their good taste. And that really comes into play whether it is a Michelangelo or a Léger or the latest work of art by the hottest contemporary painter. No matter what the aesthetic merits of a particular piece are, decisions are made in purely monetary terms as well. People ask themselves, "Should I or shouldn't I buy it?"

Q: How has your experience as an art dealer confirmed your sense that determination of value is a relative concept?

ALAN: Bob, I think it gets to the very heart of what money is. Money is just money until it's converted into some assets. Whether it is a home or a car. The thing is that you can accumulate just so much money. As far as I can tell, after you have achieved a certain level of financial security, money's only purpose is to enhance the quality of your life. That is basically the nature of the business that I'm in. At this level it's not about having people come in and be shoppers! We're not selling art like they do in a shopping mall. We're selling art to very sophisticated clients who want to understand the context of the art—to recognize the aesthetic values in order to enhance their personal values and enrich their individual experience. I don't know if that sounds a little too pompous!

Q: It sounds as though you're selling imagination.
ALAN: Well, in some sense, I guess we are.

AESTHETIC VALUES

Q: Alan, what do you think your experience as a professional trader and now as an art dealer has taught you about value?

ALAN: I guess one thing that I learned initially from trading is that price is merely a perception of value. Values change constantly: in monetary terms and aesthetic terms. At particular periods, certain aesthetic values are in and others are out of favor. The important point is, what you have to find is a work of art that has meaning for you as an individual, that holds value for you. You must feel it will enhance your life and experience. That can only come from you, not from a dealer telling you certain works of art will "light up your life."

Q: Alan, as it relates to value and money, what do you think you learned most about yourself?

ALAN: I know now that money can't be the be-all and end-all to one's life. And it might sound really trite, but the truth of the matter is, for most people it is. And they might say it's not but they pay a heavy price for living in big houses and driving expensive cars. I've learned that I'm most happy doing what I'm doing right now, engaged in the life that I chose for myself as opposed to the life that I felt that I had to pursue to gratify others. I lived the first 43 years of my life proving to my parents I could be successful. From here on out it's all for me and my family. Occasionally, I look at the markets and I think about a particular trade. Then I turn around and look on my gallery walls and see a painting by Picasso or a sculpture by Calder or a photograph by Stieglitz or Steichen and I sigh a huge sigh of relief. I'm glad that other life has passed!

CHAPTER 29

Worshiping the Almighty Dollar

Dr. Joseph Morgan

JOSEPH MORGAN, MD, 41, works as a part-time consultant to pharmaceutical companies. He gave up his full-time position to spend more time with his family.

Q: Joseph, what is your earliest memory of money?

JOSEPH: Something I was aware that my family did not have a lot of. Even coins counted. Money was something that my parents both worked very hard for. And it was not something to be wasted, because we didn't have enough to waste.

Q: Did both of your parents work?

JOSEPH: Yes. My father, a Holocaust survivor, had two jobs. He was a personnel manager of a small company during the regular workweek, and he also taught Hebrew school on Sunday to supplement his income. My mother, who came to the United States in 1922 because of the civil war in Russia, worked as a medical secretary. She worked less than full-time so she could leave for work when I went to school and then she could return around the time I arrived home. My parents separated when I was about two years old, and my father provided limited child support.

Q: As you were growing up, what were your thoughts about money?

JOSEPH: Money was something that in our immediate family we did not have a lot of. But I was also aware of a relative who was considered very wealthy, even a millionaire, and other relatives who were very solidly in the middle class. They helped my mother and me financially and emotionally from childhood through medical school, and later in their wills. As I was growing up, money was both very important and something that we were lacking in our family. But interestingly, I didn't bear the brunt of its absence in my family. In other words there was certainly enough to eat. My parents didn't scrimp when it came to feeding me or educating me. I clearly understood that when they were growing up, it was under conditions of near starvation in Eastern Europe.

Q: As an adolescent, do you remember having any particular fantasies that revolved around money?

JOSEPH: When I was a teenager I had a lot of friends who lived in the suburbs. One of my fantasies was to imagine what it would be like to have a house in the suburbs with a backyard and a car. Of course, we didn't have a car. Bob, I should point out that right now I live in that house about which I fantasized.

Q: You currently live in the house of your fantasy?

JOSEPH: Right, my exact childhood fantasy. A nice new house with a creek and woods in our backyard out in the suburbs with a wife, three little kids, and two cars.

Q: Joseph, how would you characterize your current relationship with money?

JOSEPH: It certainly has evolved over time and it's still evolving. I used to be a lot more anxious about money than I am now because I used to be afraid of everything being taken away from me. I now look at money as if it's not the most important thing in life, although there are a lot of people who think it is. My feeling is they're worshiping a false god, as I once worshiped that same false god.

Q: In what sense did you worship money and what led to your viewing it differently?

JOSEPH: I once believed that the goal of adult life, aside from marriage and having children, was to make as much money as possible. And that through making money, one achieved security and one had a comfortable life and possibly could even undo some of the feelings of not having money while growing up.

Q: Do you mean that money could somehow undo some psychological feeling of insufficiency?

JOSEPH: Oh, I really believed that for a very long time! I'd say for probably 10 to 15 years of my adulthood, especially during my peak earning years. I really believed that and it was one of the reasons why I worked so hard.

Q: What has changed your thinking?

JOSEPH: I realized that the more I had, the more I wanted. And that with more money as the goal, one could never reach the goal. And I was always aware that instead of enjoying what I had, I was distressed over what I didn't yet have or what insufficiency I perceived as a result of comparing myself with others who had more. Over time I began to realize how thankful I am for what I have achieved and how much I enjoy what I have. Currently, I do not live at my means: I live far below my means. And worshiping money—which was once kind of my goal without realizing it as such—is for me, now, something I consider a negative value.

Q: To what extent do you feel others define you in terms of how much money you have?

JOSEPH: Well, this is the essence of secular American middle-class culture, being defined by how much money you have or the kind of car you drive or the clothes you wear. I think for people who don't know you, this is how they very rapidly define and categorize you.

I should also mention that although I grew up at the end of the '60s, I was very sympathetic to hippie cuture. Particularly with wearing jeans and flannel shirts and army surplus, because that whole issue of dress—in terms of looking at the person and not at the externals—I believe made a significant antiestablishment statement.

Q: To what extent do you feel that you define yourself in terms of how much money you have? How are your feelings of self-esteem tied to money?

JOSEPH: I would have had a very different answer to this question even six months ago and may have a different answer to it six months from now. I've come to realize that security comes from God and not from chasing money. And I mean that in a very powerful sense. I can't believe how much money I'm making now and the kind of lifestyle that I live. It's kind of at the level of fantasy that I had for myself when I was growing up. And chasing more of it has caused me only anxiety. So I'm quite satisfied with what my family has and with what we're saving and investing. I don't work as much or as hard as I used to and I really like having time during the day to do other things, like riding a bike or studying philosophy—especially Hasidic philosophy. In the past I would have looked at every moment I was not earning maximum dollars as time wasted, including time spent with my own children. Now I look at work as a part-time chore. It is not an end in itself, to make as much money as possible. That is why I only work two days a week now.

Q: What is most valuable for you today and why?

JOSEPH: I'm not sure that I could answer what's most valuable. But among the valuable things are meaningful interactions with my wife and with my children. Also studying Hasidic philosophy, especially the writings of my relatives. Feeling that I'm really growing in my awareness of God in all aspects in life. And a particularly valuable thing is really feeling the changes that I'm making in my own personality and character to make them more pleasant for myself and for others. In particular, I'm not as self-centered as I used to be.

Q: This strong belief in God that you mentioned has that helped you balance your perspective about money?

JOSEPH: Absolutely. And it's really made me think about and change my values and priorities from the absolute tangible in the form of gold or money to the eternal and the spiritual. And that's very difficult to talk about, the sensation of awareness of God and awareness of value systems far superior to that of the pursuit of money as something to be worshiped.

Q: Joseph, in your universe of values, what do you think is the ultimate purpose of money?

JOSEPH: I'm not sure if money has only a single purpose. The spiritual goal and purpose is to advance godliness. It's almost easier to answer that in terms of what is not the purpose of money than what is. Having said that, the practical purpose of money is to facilitate and simplify material transactions. But what money isn't, is clear: it's not something to be hoarded, it's not something to be worshiped and it's not an end in itself. It's something that exists in our world and to the extent that we value it and do things with it that are in themselves positive values, we are living higher-quality and more spiritual lives.

Q: To what extent do you think money has significantly affected the quality of your life?

JOSEPH: Well, materially I'm raising my children in far more comfort and luxury than the environment that I grew up in. We did not have a car when I was growing up. My parents and I took public transportation and they purposely bought a house on a major bus line (the "C" bus in the Logan section of Philadelphia) for easy transportation to other parts of the city. My wife and I each have our own automobile that was something, when I was growing up, that only the very wealthy could afford. At the same time, we wish we had a three-car garage instead of a two-car garage because we could use more storage space!

Q: Materialism creeps in even in the form of an extra garage, right?

JOSEPH: I'm not knocking materialism at all. It's the worship of materialism as an end in itself and the valuation of others and the assessment of others solely in material terms that I think is really a negative value: slavery to money no matter how much you have. It's really a frame of reference that I've changed for myself from a completely money-oriented one to a more spiritual one.

Q: What do you think it is about money that hangs us up so, both individually and as a society?

JOSEPH: In our society, awareness of God is generally at a very low level and awareness of materialism is at a very high level. I think in our parents' and our grandparents' generations, regardless of your religion or ethnic background, the opposite was true. Also, at a time of unprecedented affluence in America, we realize that having more money doesn't necessarily make us more satisfied. We can have an incredibly fancy meal at an elegant restaurant and feel really terrific for half an hour, but so what? That indulgence is quickly forgotten. Money becomes almost like a drug. And if you keep on doing it to feel that high, then you're going to weigh 300 pounds and have a cholesterol level of 300 and risk a premature death. So I think that what we're really doing is challenging our values and priorities as individuals and as a nation, but we're doing it very privately—certainly not yet in the public arena. I think the very fact that you're writing this book and there's so much interest in coming to terms with money and wealth is a reflection of the fact that we're really questioning in our own minds what our values should be as they relate to money.

Q: Joseph, what do you think is the most important thing you learned about yourself?

JOSEPH: The pursuit of money and my own anxiety were very closely related. The more money I had, the more anxious I became about it being taken away. Therefore, changing my reference from one of worshiping money to pursuing more positive values—spending more time with my family, studying sacred literature with a Hasidic rabbi, reassessing my own priorities, and focusing on spiritual issues—has ironically afforded me the security I was so desperately looking for. I've learned in the final analysis that security has less to do with money and more to do with acknowledging God and understanding yourself. "To thine own self be true."

CHAPTER 30

Believing Is Seeing

Barbara Holt

Ms. Barbara Holt is an alderman from the Fifth Ward on Chicago's South Side.

Q: What is your earliest memory of money?

Barbara: I grew up in poverty. My earliest memory of money is the constant lack of it and the struggle to acquire it to secure basic needs. My family lived in a kitchenette apartment and I remember this constant conflict between my parents about money. My mother worked in a laundry. Before that she had worked as a domestic. It seemed to me she always worked very far away, and she had to leave home very early. My father worked sporadically in various occupations, and what I remember is their arguments about money. We used to have these poker games, and that was a way to make money, too.

Q: In your family's home?

Barbara: Yes, like Saturday night poker games, and they would cut the pot.

Q: Kind of like a rent party, something like that?

Barbara: Well, yes, the same kind of concept.

Q: Do you remember your parents having a particular attitude toward money as you were growing up?

BARBARA: Yes. This is something I came to realize only later, but it's all tied to a sense of self-esteem. My mother had a very low sense of self-esteem and this all relates to my family's attitude toward money. When you asked me that question, a particular memory came up. It was my third or fourth birthday and my parents had a party for me. We played things like Pin the Tail on the Donkey and other traditional games. The winners got prizes. And I recall that I won a game and got this prize, and my mother insisted that I give it back because she said it wasn't right for me to win because it was my party. I realized later in life that that was a really significant occurrence for me. I realized I had internalized this event to mean that I was not worthy to have what I wanted.

There was something else. My birthday is January 11. My mother would tell people at Christmas time that I was supposed to have been born on Christmas Day, and since I was born on January 11, only three weeks later, she told them that they didn't have to give me anything for my birthday if they gave me a Christmas present. I know that my mother meant well, but she obviously had a really deep-seated feeling of limitation that was reflected in our economic condition. Of course, in this society, money is the major mechanism for getting the material things that you want.

Q: So, Barbara, what do you think you learned from these experiences?

BARBARA: What I learned, and didn't recognize I was learning, was "impossibility." What was communicated at that time was that you can't have what you want in life, and money is something that people want. She was conveying the idea of limitation. There was another message she gave me, too, and that was that I shouldn't want to have money. And that I should be satisfied with the hand-me-down clothes that she would bring home from the family she worked for. There was a daughter in the family who was older than me and my mother would bring her clothes home. The message to me was very clear: I shouldn't want anything better!

Q: As you were growing up, did you have any particular thoughts or fantasies about money?

BARBARA: I wanted to live differently. Initially I wasn't exposed to people living what you'd call a middle-class or upper-middle-class life. But I knew from images on television and in magazines that some people did live differently. I just don't think I really saw it as a possibility for myself.

Q: Barbara, could you talk a little bit about how your early childhood and adolescent experiences have influenced your career choice, and how they've shaped your current attitude toward money?

BARBARA: My early experience influenced my commitment to changing society so that no one has to live in poverty. I believe that we're wealthy enough as a society so that it is a real possibility. Of course, that requires some reordering of priorities. I also have to weave into this commitment my own philosophy and what I believe money represents.

I think we can look at money as energy, that is, energy made manifest. So if you've internalized the belief that money is scarce, and that there's got to be competition between people for it, then that's going to be the inevitable consequence. I always go back to the story of the Puritans. John Winthrop was leading the group and he spoke to them on the *Arabella* in order to prepare people for the New World. He told them not to expect equality in the New World. He told them how wealth and poverty were predetermined, and how some would always be poor. I think that we, too, have internalized that idea. As I look at where I am today and my experience of having grown up in poverty, I know that I have to break that connection and we also have to do that as a society. That's one of the reasons why I want to effect change not just of political policies and practices, but of more fundamental things:

how people internalize their experiences in their minds and their hearts.

Q: So, what you're saying is that one of your goals is to transform the way people think about wealth and value in their lives. Is that correct?

BARBARA: Yes.

Q: Could you talk a little bit more about that in specific terms, like what you find yourself having to do in order to bring about that transformation?

BARBARA: Yes, let me see if I can explain this. I should add this thought process is still evolving in terms of my own thinking, but I have studied the workings of the mind and belief systems, and this is certainly not conventional in the circles of politics and government.

Q: Right, I don't think this is the perspective of most Chicago aldermen.

BARBARA: No, it is not. I think what I do is bring a different perspective to the table. I came to this work with an idea that I wanted to change things, not that I wanted to go into a system and be a part of it. I find the most frustrating part of my work is to participate in the passage of legislation. For example, I don't think the way to solve the crime issue is by hiring more police or building more prisons. What we need to do is transform attitudes in order to effect meaningful change.

Let me see if I can give you an example. Where my office is located at 71st and Constance, there's a lot of drug activity. There's also prostitution. I see people who appear to be totally lost in life and who are struggling for money to support a particular habit, which translates into high rates of crime. There's an elderly woman who was just attacked going into her garage last week. The criminals who robbed her left her for dead in a ravine. They were seeking money to support their drug addiction! Now, how do we change those kinds of behaviors? That's the fundamental question I have to ask myself. I've used visualization to change attitudes or to help people accomplish things. I have used Michael Jordan or other sports heros as motivational images, because people seem to accept it more naturally. I believe we can work with people and teach them some of these techniques that allow them to change their lives inwardly. And that is how I want to approach change. I can't always do it overtly in the political arena that I'm in, but through individual interactions with my colleagues and with constituents, I can bring this idea to the people I serve.

Someone recently told me about a study that was done in a prison. Inmates were taught to visualize what they were going to do when they get out of jail. As you know the recidivism rate of violent criminals is very high and part of the problem is that most offenders can't see themselves leaving prison and living successful lives on the outside, free of criminal activity. In this study, however, the experimental group was taught to visualize themselves being successful outside of prison. They found the recidivism rate was significantly lower. Now, that sounds touchy-feely or New Age, but I believe these programs do work!

Q: I think, Barbara, the concept of change as you have expressed it is really a very interesting and practical concept. It seems to me as I look at the lives and the attitudes of people who live day in and day out in poverty, what has always struck me most profoundly was not their lack of material objects, but the poverty of constructive attitudes: belief in themselves and the larger society. People begin to internalize a psychologically damaging vision of themselves. To the extent that we can radically affect the way people see themselves as individuals and as members of mainstream society—of course getting the larger society to view the disenfranchised as members of the American family is also called for— the greater our chances of building a more productive nation as well as one that is fundamentally more humane.

BARBARA: That's a good point, Bob, that it's not just the people who are in poverty who have to do this, it's also everybody else! We don't have to view society as competitive.

Q: You know, Barbara, when it comes to poverty of vision, there's a lot to go around. Why haven't we realized that we are all part of the whole? The idea of competition I think is also quite interesting. On one extreme there are winners and on the other there are losers. If you choose to see society that way, then all the glory goes to the victors, and somehow the losers—because they haven't measured up—by their very circumstances justify their condition.

BARBARA: That does seem to be the prevailing view.

Q: Yeah, well, if poor people somehow would just pull themselves up by their bootstraps, you know, everything would be hunky-dory!

BARBARA: I think that's right, but not in the way that the conservatives view it.

Q: So how do we ultimately change the way people think about values?

BARBARA: Let's start with the idea that every moment you have a choice, that's the ultimate power. And things may be going on around you, but what becomes of you is up to you, you know? There's another concept that is essential to understand and that is to be able to *respond* rather than to *react*. Response involves a conscious choice. So when we encounter stimuli that the most valuable thing in the world is possessing a lot of money or having material possessions, it is important to know that we have a choice in how we respond.

I think you have to have a leadership, someone standing up and saying, OK, you can approach these issues differently. I have problems with a lot of the analysis that goes on: a lot of the rhetoric that we hear about the plight of the poor—and the plight of African-

BELIEVING IS SEEING

Americans in particular—is what I call victim analysis. If you say that you're in this situation because someone else has the power to put you there, then you can never get to the point where you will have the power to get out because power to do so is outside of you. And that is why I like the perspective of people like Les Brown who popularized some of the ideas we are speaking about.

Q: Live your dreams.

BARBARA: Right. There are a number of people who are working at various levels to convey to people that you can change your life by starting from within. There's the classic self-help book, *Think and Grow Rich*, by Napoleon Hill. It came out in the '40s or '50s. Wayne Dyer has a recent book titled *You'll See When You Believe It*. So there's a lot of this type of material around.

Q: What you're really saying, Barbara, is that one's poverty, in the final analysis, is an outgrowth of one's state of mind. Is that correct?

BARBARA: Well, that's my belief, and I always think about the quote from Eleanor Roosevelt, who said, "No one can make you feel inferior without your consent."

Q: Barbara, as it relates to the whole issue of money and value, what did you learn most about yourself?

BARBARA: I've learned that money is a physical manifestation of where people are in their consciousnesses. Money is a symbol of supply in one's life. It is a reflection of fundamental beliefs about oneself. I've also learned, and I mentioned it at the beginning concerning my family's struggles with money, to stop struggling and to learn to trust. When I decided to run for office, I had no financial base, I had no organization. I actually sat at my dining room table and just called people I knew. Ultimately to run the campaign cost about $80,000. And it involved some debt, but I saw that if I was determined, we could raise the money and that I could accomplish my goal. It had to do with consciousness and that is what I'm trying to get across to my constituents.

Q: So what you learned basically was that where there is a will, there's a way, and that you wouldn't allow the money to become an obstacle in achieving your vision of yourself and your community. Is that right?

BARBARA: That's right. I think the key is to focus on purpose. There's a book that I read titled *Do What You Love and the Money Will Follow* by Marsha Sinetar. The idea is that if you focus on what you truly want to achieve in life, the monetary part takes care of itself. In my experience, that is true!

CHAPTER 31

Money Matters:

I Did It for the Money

> With money in your pocket you are wise, and you are handsome, and you sing well, too.
>
> —*Yiddish proverb*

In the ancient Greek myth, Dionysius grants King Midas exactly what he desires more than anything else in the world: the ability to turn everything he touches into gold. Midas exclaims ecstatically, "I am the richest man in the world; the happiest man in the world!" It is only when the king reaches out to touch the daughter he loves so much that he realizes tragic implications he had failed to consider.

I believe most Americans operate from a belief system that our financial life, that is our attitudes about wealth and money, are somehow divorced from the other parts of our lives—separate from our values and purpose. Nothing could be further from the truth! The way we internalize the meaning of money, as we have seen in the interviews, has profound and unforeseen implications:

- The attitudes we have about money encompasses far more than just our earnings, savings, spending, and debt.
- Money is reflected in the sense of satisfaction and fulfillment we derive from our families, our communities, and our professions.
- For many Americans, money is a pernicious litmus test of personal identity and self-worth.

- To a large extent our childhood and adolescent experiences with money drive our later decisions about wealth and value.
- What is of greatest value to us as individuals is often directly related to our psychological concepts of wealth and money.

Consider the following:

- Art historian Tom Cummins left the family bond business where he could have made millions to live among indigenous people in South America. In the midst of harsh poverty and economic hyperinflation, he observes human conditions that teach him something valuable about himself and the meaning of wealth.
- Cook County Judge Michele Lowrance witnesses ugly and costly family disputes, revolving around issues of child custody, divorce, and estate settlements, and concludes that the ultimate value of money is to form meaningful relationships with others in order to find personal fulfillment and "leave a positive imprint."
- Criminal defense attorney Matt Mahoney observes on a daily basis the crude and lethal extremes people go to secure money. "They don't kill out of desperation even, it's just blatant and deliberate greed." Despite this observation, he has moved from being a state prosecutor to a defense lawyer. However he still finds himself identifying with "the good guys." He also cites that the strongest influences for the development of his own values was his father, a former CIA agent, who "taught me to act out of principle not for monetary gains."
- Office manager Donna Hughes simplified her life and attitudes about money when she accepted Jesus into her life. She continues to work at arm's-length distance from her boss, one of the most successful commodity traders in the

country, whose daily market swings involve hundreds of thousands of dollars.
- Artist Dorian Sylvain acknowledges the rampant materialism and consumerism of the American economy. There is unfortunately an all-too-common "La Vie Bohême" psychology among artists that somehow they need to starve to be successful. Dorian is struck by the irony that artists need to be paid more for their work, but at the same time wants prices to be "affordable" so she can pursue her passion for collecting art. "We should all have access to wonderful works of art. They should not be deposited into the hands and homes of a wealthy few."
- Astronomer Edward Kibblewhite views money and finance as "a crashing bore." However, he admits his professional ranking at the University of Chicago is, to a large extent, evaluated on how much grant money he can generate.
- Cambridge-trained economist Judith McCue feels "I have been irresponsible when it has come to thinking critically about money." For her, money was something to be thought about in the abstract. "I may know all about a country's gross national product and yet I have never been able to effectively balance my own personal checkbook."
- Professional gambler John Monasta plays blackjack and trades S&P futures because they give him a feeling of security. He doesn't feel he is engaging in risky behavior, because "when I play, I just know that I'm going to win."
- Dr. Joyce Rubin who, although she could well afford it, feels stressfully guilty when purchasing new clothing for herself, as if she is violating a long-established family value.
- Cancer specialist Michele Carbone feels, as a result of his experience with the patients he treats in his practice, "That financial security is a very insecure concept."
- David Held, a successful Eurodollar broker whose childhood fantasy was to have enough money to retire so that he

could spend his time fishing, now owns a home on the bank of a lake.
- Clinton Secret Service agent Rich Buendorf observed the untoward effects of money on the presidency. He retired from the Secret Service to start his own foundation to aid impoverished inner-city dwellers. His goal is to change the substandard housing conditions of poor people throughout the country.
- Asset Management Company president Larry Rosenberg, who admits to "having had it all" and "living the American dream to the fullest," has adopted a lifestyle of simplicity. He sold most of his material possessions, including his cars. He places emphasis on the point that "when you have money, it is a responsibility and an obligation to help others."
- Geneticist Carole Ober, who has studied and lived among the Hutterites, found that their rejection of individual ownership and commitment to collective living provides them with a rich system of personal and societal values that is sorrowfully missing in the general culture. She finds it interesting that her own rejection of "financial matters" has led her to her life's work.
- Psychiatrist and rabbi Abraham Twerski feels he is still trying to measure up to his family's rabbinical tradition of *zedakah* (charity for the needy—where all wealth is destined for that purpose). He is concerned with the contemporary life he lives in the context of Halakic (biblical) imperatives regarding money. As the founder of one of the most successful drug rehabilitation programs in the country, the Gateway Rehabilitating Centers, he is a strong advocate for a new system of values that concentrates on the pursuit of meaning in one's life, rather than the pursuit of pleasure. "Money, like alcohol or crack cocaine, can never provide the fulfillment and satisfaction its users are after." Ironically, his own personal crisis at the age of 38 revolved around

issues of self-esteem and external values (i.e., wealth and status) leading him to his current professional interest.
- Inner-city alderman Barbara Holt's monetarily deprived childhood solidified her belief that poverty is as much a psychological state of consciousness as it is a condition of economic life. She still remembers the experiences of her overworked and underpaid laundress mother and the effect that experience had on the family and Barbara's personal concept of self-worth. She encourages Chicago's fifth-ward residents to take personal responsibility for their lives and not view themselves as victims. She is a strong advocate for recognizing the rich cultural contributions and resources of her impoverished constituents. She encourages a new definition of wealth in America.
- Young entrepreneur Kenny Dichter is at the threshold of becoming a millionaire, selling his start-up company to a major multimedia corporation. For him money is just a way of keeping score.
- Nebraska dentist Earl Augspurger was on track to being in the upper echelon of AT&T management at the age of 33, but went back to school to become a dentist to secure a career where he could spend more time with his wife and family.
- Art gallery owner Alan Koppel made a dramatic life and career change at the age of 45. "The first 45 years of my life were concerned with living up to my parents' expectations—the right house, cars, profession!" Ironically he observes being an art dealer is almost exactly like his first career, trading financial and agricultural derivatives. "Art, like pork bellies or soybeans, is valued on the basis of perception. It is not what an artwork is inherently worth, but what it is perceived to be worth. Why else would someone pay $84 million for a Van Gogh painting that never sold in the lifetime of the artist?"

- Private investigator Paul Ciolino has provided security and investigative services for some of the world's wealthiest individuals, among them the Prince of Brunei. He finds wealth at this level surreal and boring. He also reflects on his success in light of his humble working-class background and a constant clientele of individuals who are in trouble with the law because they have chosen "shortcuts."
- Pastor Jim Nicodem views people's attitudes toward money as a window to their souls and admits to the tension in his own life of balancing his suburban lifestyle with the Christian ideal. He also struggles with being too judgmental about those who don't contribute generously to support the church's work.
- *Chicago Tribune* reporter Stephen Franklin, raised by his postal worker father, learned at an early age to rely on himself and to be an advocate for the less fortunate. A stint in the Peace Corps and working in a penal institution confirmed his belief that "having less money and less power in America means you will be blamed for all sorts of things because of your economic condition." His commitment to being a champion for the downtrodden is not without its irony. Stephen continues to be amazed that his paper pays him handsomely for his writing. "I don't do it for the money, I would keep doing this job even if they didn't pay me at all."

As each of us considers the meaning of money in our own lives, I think it serves us well to ask ourselves these questions:

- What is my earliest memory of money?
- What was my family's attitude toward money?
- Where did I develop my current attitudes toward money?
- How do these attitudes affect my thoughts and behaviors when it comes to money?

- How is my current career consistent or inconsistent with my beliefs about money and my personal system of values?
- How would I characterize my current relationship with money?
- To what extent do I allow others or myself to define me in terms of money?
- What is most valuable to me?
- To what extent do I allow money, rather than relationships, to significantly affect the quality of my life?
- What is it about money that hangs me up?
- As it relates to money, what have I learned most about myself?

Clarifying our personal attitudes about money is fundamental: it involves emotional, moral, and practical judgments about what's truly important to each of us. I believe they involve judgments directly relating to what makes life worth living. Why else would one person jump out of a high-rise office building after a stock market crash, while another renounces all material possessions and takes an oath of poverty in order to work with the world's less fortunate.

I speak to this issue not as someone who has achieved definitive answers but rather as a fellow traveler in search of clarity. Walter D. Staples writes, "when you change your thinking, you change your beliefs; when you change your beliefs, you change your expectations; when you change your expectations, you change your attitudes; when you change your attitudes, you change your behavior; when you change your behavior, you change your performance; when you change your performance, you change your life!" It is important to remember that in relation to money and the material environment we live in, much is still within our control:

- We can control our thinking if we take the time to become aware of the thoughts we are processing and assume responsibility for them.
- We can control our beliefs and the way we imagine ourselves.
- We can control the way we conceptualize the world and visualize our place and future in it.
- We can control the goals we set for ourselves and the steps to take in order to achieve them.
- We can control the way we allocate our time and the way we spend our day.
- We can control what is important to us, with whom we associate, and the focus of our attention.
- We can affect the environment we learn and live in.
- We can control our response to situations and circumstances that influence our thinking and behavior.
- We can control the intensity, fun, and desire we bring to all our efforts.

In their book, *Your Money or Your Life,* Joe Dominguez and Vicki Robin suggest that the way most Americans navigate their financial lives is based on an old road map. They write:

> Even though we "won" the industrial revolution, the spoils of war are looking more and more spoiled. This is especially true for us as individuals. The old road map for money has us trapped in the very vehicle that was supposed to liberate us from toil... Our old financial map, instead of making us more independent, fulfilled individuals, has led us into a web of financial dependence.... The material progress that was supposed to free us has left us more enslaved.

It seems clear that there is a compelling need to chart a new road map for money and what we as individuals value. It begins with identifying what is truly important to us. It involves understanding our motives and motivations for securing money, knowing our personal "financial" belief systems, and reevaluating the strategies and behaviors we adopt to reach our goals. It is interesting to note again just how psychological a concept money truly is.

Money is not something external to ourselves! If you still harbor any doubt whatsoever, just consider the words we attribute to money:

- Hope
- Power
- Success
- Security
- Acceptance
- Fulfillment
- Happiness
- Achievement
- Personal worth

Money is inextricably attached to our psyche like financial Velcro, affecting our thoughts, beliefs, attitudes, and dreams—even the American dream. We are locked in a struggle to find out where does it stop and where do we begin. We have unconsciously given over so much power to it that it has become the master and we the slaves. Ironically, this occurs both passively—through disinterest and denial, and actively—through committing to accumulate as much money as possible. Larry Rosenberg said it quite well when he observed, "The more money I acquired, the less money I felt I had. The more possessions I accumulated, the more I felt possessed. In the end I felt money was the victor and I was the vanquished."

Money becomes money only at the instant it incorporates a wish; and I saw that it was a treadmill, that it led us all on a mad bacchanal from which we could not break out and sit down.

—*James Buchan*

Themes from the Interviews

Money is not buying us the happiness we seek. It is quite clear from the interviews that beyond a minimum level of comfort, money does not provide the fulfillment we are seeking. A new Lexus or Infinity or the toy of our choice provides little more than a distraction from what we truly seem to be searching for: purpose in our lives. Ironically, money does not bring about an enriched life. We have to find practical and dynamic ways to enhance our ability to attain meaning and value in our work, families, and community.

We cling to our affluence out of insecurity. Our affluent lifestyles are having an increasingly devastating effect on our personal and national lives. Our collective mania for newer, faster, and better material objects depletes our physical and spiritual energy. Consumerism not only threatens our natural resources, but widens the serious gulf between rich and poor. The past decade has seen a concentration of wealth that is unprecedented in this century. Add to this dynamic the ever-present media hype of individual inefficiency and the need for newer luxuries juxtaposed with homelessness and chronic poverty. Poor people are justifiably envious and angry. Millions are homeless and seek affordable housing. Inner-city residents, as well as middle-class families in suburbs, feel as though they are working harder and longer hours than ever before. In the past decade the United States has gone from the largest creditor nation to the world's largest debtor nation. We sense a collective uneasiness that we are on the threshold of a dramatic turning point. Financially, socially, politically, and spiritually, we sense there is a better way.

We do not feel as though we have all that much to show for our money. It is remarkable how this theme kept coming up. There was a basic belief in the "poverty of affluence and a disbelief in the idea of financial security." Material affluence is seen by many as an active agent deleteriously affecting our spiritual fiber. Its effects range from substance abuse to a generalized feeling of anxiety and despair. As Howard Abell said, "If you live for having it all, what you have is never enough." In *Your Money or Your Life,* Joe Dominguez and Vicki Robin write, "For all the hype about going for the gold, we're so weary at the end of the day that going for the sofa is as good as it gets."

We need to simplify our individual lives and reevaluate our national priorities when it comes to money. There is a general recognition that "we are not our jobs." We come home at the end of our workday with tired bodies and empty souls. The common explanation to excuse this condition is the familiar "I do it for the money." However, more and more we are beginning to recognize the need for a new road map. In this regard it is helpful to remind ourselves that any map is not the territory! But even so, psychologically, emotionally, and spiritually we want more than to have to "owe our soul to the company store." There is a growing understanding that simplifying our lives can come about through recognizing the inextricable role that our attitudes about money and wealth exercise on the quality of our individual experience.

It is also understood that there is a need for an attitudinal change in the larger culture. As Dorian Sylvain asked rhetorically, "What kind of long-lasting message do our children get from MTV and Calvin Klein ads?" I think it is quite appropriate to tell our children without equivocation that "enough is enough." There is also the need to form interest groups and elect candidates who forward that message. I think it is perfectly legitimate to send out a clear and strong message that materialism helps, but it also hurts! Continuing in the current direction seriously threatens our country's moral and spiritual health.

We do not have to sit by passively. Each of us can effect change. Although it is clear that we often harbor conflicting and contradictory beliefs about the role of money in our lives, each of us has the capability to influence change in the way we think about money and the actions we take. Each of us can, in our own way, emulate Peter Finch in the movie *Network* and say, "I'm mad as hell and I'm not going to take it anymore." In fact, we see dramatic examples of that throughout the interviews.

As individuals we have tremendous power to change ourselves and our society: we can bring a deeper purpose into our lives and that of others. I believe it is only as a result of being able to identify with a higher, positive purpose—whether it is God, conducting cancer research, fostering humanitarian work, or just maintaining the belief that you are making a meaningful contribution—that we can attain the feeling of happiness we so desperately and incorrectly attribute to money. It is an immense journey. Each of us in our own way can be one of a chorus of voices that resonates for good.

Change requires in many ways making visible the invisible, discovering new patterns of meaning in our lives that uncover unforeseen personal values. Change means taking our intuitive dreams and wishes seriously and looking beyond the omnipresent muddle and meaningless confusion of vulgar materialism and conspicuous consumption. Change also means having the courage to be persistent in our conviction to make a difference, to be stubborn in our belief that the meaning of money is not external to us. Value does not reside in precious metals, bank notes, or electronic impulses. Value lives within each of us according to the importance we assign to it. I believe for too long we have assigned too much value

MONEY MATTERS: I DID IT FOR THE MONEY

to money, making it more important than our greatest resource: human life itself. Depending on our attitudes and intentions, money can be used as a rich energy flow that transforms and purifies each one of us so that the dividend of what we discover in ourselves can be shared by all of society; or money's energy can be a stagnant—even toxic—charge of self-centeredness and greed that contaminates our worldview. We can be either slaves or masters, victors or vanquished.

In *Man's Search for Meaning,* Viktor Frankl writes, "It did not matter what we expected from life, but rather what life expected from us . . . we needed to stop asking about the meaning of life but instead to think of ourselves as those who were being questioned by life, daily and hourly."

It is within our power to influence money's complex course and direction; to keep it flowing where it can do the most work enhancing and fulfilling the positive in human life. That may be money's ultimate purpose, where it gets its full value. When money talks, we should listen.

Index

A

Abell, Howard, 180-86
Addiction, 162
Affluence and spirituality, 243. *See also* Spirituality
Alachem, Shalom, 7
Allen, Woody, iii
American culture, and money, 26-29, 40-41, 48, 50, 55-56, 82, 128-29, 158, 163-65, 192, 196, 223
    vs. Great Britain, 207-8
Anabaptists, 154
Anxiety, about money, 25-30
Art, buying, 215-16
Arts Presenting in Education, 74
Asian market panic, 7
Association for the Advancement of Creative Musicians, 74
Attitudes, toward money, 233, 238-39
Augspurger, Earl, 146-49, 237

B

Baldwin, James, 5
Barnum, P. T., 14
Billings, Josh, 6
Boesky, Ivan, 6
Bohn, Henry George, 7
Book titles, money themes, 8
Buchan, James, 2, 242
Buchan, John, iv
Buendorf, Rich, 60-69, 236

C

Camus, Albert, 193
Capitalism, 82
Carbone, Michele, 194-98, 235
Casino Gambler's Guide, The, 111
Change, capability of, 244-45
Charity, 159-60, 166
Childhood experiences, with money, 234
Ciolino, Paul, 199-205, 238
Clinton, Bill, 61-64
Cohen, Myron, 14
Consumerism, 48-50, 105, 128-29, 163, 196, 242
Control, of money and environment, 239-40
Corporate culture, 48-49
Csikszentmihalyi, Mihaly, 22
cummings, e.e., 1, 210
Cummins, Tom, 173-79, 234

INDEX

D

Dearborn Financial Publishing, 11
Dichter, Kenny, 131-36, 237
Dohrn, Bernadine, 100-107
Dominguez, Joe, 240, 243
Do What You Love and the Money Will Follow, 232
Dyer, Wayne, 231

E

Eliot, T. S., 24
Emerson, Ralph Waldo, 6

F

Fear, and money, 118-19
Finch, Peter, 244
Fletcher, Cybil, 5
Flow: The Psychology of Optimal Experience, 22
Frankl, Viktor, 23, 245
Franklin, Benjamin, 6
Franklin, Stephen, 187-93, 238
Frost, Robert, iii
Frozen Desire, 2

G

Gambling, professional, 110-12, 116
Gateway Rehabilitating Centers, 236
Geffen, David, 135
Generosity, 129
Getty, J. Paul, iii
Grant, James, 106
Grants, academic, 153-54
Greed, 34-37, 201-2, 208-9
Greeley, Horace, iv

H

Hamlet, xii
Happiness, and money, 242
Hasidic values, 164
Held, David, 168-72, 235-36

Hill, Napoleon, 231
Holt, Barbara, 225-32, 237
Horace, 6
Hughes, Donna, 85-91, 234
Hunt, Bunker, 81
Hutterites, 154-57

I

Insecurity, and need for money, 242
Instant gratification, 41

J

Jones, Grant, 77-84
Journalists, 191-92

K

Kibblewhite, Edward, 206-11, 235
Koppel, Alan, 212-17, 237-38
Koppel, Robert, 15-24

L

"Little Gidding," 24
Louis, Joe, 15
Lowrance, Michele, 117-24, 234

M

Mahoney, Matt, 31-41, 234
Man's Search for Meaning, 23, 245
Materialism, 82, 90, 105, 163, 165, 192, 196, 223, 243
    media and, 49-50
McCue, Judith, 25-30, 235
Media, and consumerism, 48-50
Mencken, H. L., 5
Monasta, John, 108-16, 235
Money
    American attitude toward. *See* American culture, and money
    concept of, 5-6
    functions of, 4

Money continued
    history of, 1-2
    perception of, and quality of life, 8. *See also* Quality of life
    psychology of, 12
    questions to consider, to clarify personal attitude toward, 238-39
    taboo of speaking of, 10-11
Morgan, Joseph, 218-24
Murchison, Clint W., 7

N

Network, 244
Nicodem, Jim, 125-30, 238

O

Ober, Carole, 150-58, 236

P

Picasso, Pablo, 1
Pirsig, Robert, 23
Proust, Marcel, 2, 17
Puritans, 227

Q

Quality of life, 47-48, 56, 97-98, 123, 134-35, 142, 162, 190

R

Rand, Ayn, iv
Religion, 87, 127-30, 221-22. *See also* Spirituality
    Hutterites, 154-57
Remembrances of Things Past, 2
Rituals, 75
Robin, Vicki, 240, 243
Roosevelt, Eleanor, 231
Rosenberg, Larry, 53-59, 236, 241
Rubin, Joyce, 137-45, 235
Rukeyser, Louis, iii

S

Sandburg, Carl, iv
Sapir, Ira, 92-99
Security, 44, 110, 116
Security and freelancing, 44-45
Self-worth, and net worth, 130, 209-10
Simplification, 243-44
Sinetar, Marsha, 232
Social inequality, 102-3, 227-28-29
Socialism, 82
Spielberg, Steven, 143
Spirituality, 122, 127-28, 221-22, 242, 243
Staples, Walter D., 239
Stein, Gertrude, 7
Stevenson, Adlai, 1
Sylvain, Dorian, 42-52, 235, 243

T

Talmud, "Ethics of our Fathers," 16
Technical Analysis of Stocks and Commodities, 9
Themes, from interviews, 242-45
Think and Grow Rich, 231
Trumbo, Dalton, iii
Twain, Mark, 1, 7
Twerski, Abraham, 159-67, 236-37

V

Value, 244-45
Vaughan, Bill, iii
Victim analysis, 231
Voltaire, 14

W

Wagner, Honus, 11
Walton, Sam, 171
Williams, Jonathan, 14
Winthrop, John, 227

INDEX

Y

You'll See When You Believe It, 231
Youngman, Henny, iv,182
Your Money or Your Life, 240, 243

Z

Zabar, Kahil El', 70-76
Zedakah, 159
Zen and the Art of Motorcycle Maintenance, 23
Zigmund, Cindy, 11-12